Reconcilable Differences

The True Story of Tom and Jolene Young

By Tami Pflum

From Tom & Jolene:
We would like to dedicate this book to our three God-given
princesses, Shelby, Shania and Shayna.

From Tami:
This book is dedicated to anyone in need of hope.
As you turn the final page, may you be
fully persuaded that
God still moves and with Him **all** things are possible!

Note from the Youngs...

This true account of our life is intended to help and encourage married or engaged couples, as well as anyone considering marriage. We want to share the good news of the Gospel—Jesus Christ and Him Crucified—and all He is able to do with a willing and submitted heart. There is no intent to hurt any family or friends by the problems from our first marriage. We own up to all our mistakes and do not cast any blame on anyone else.

Where there is life, there is HOPE. Do not give up. Take courage and trust in an Almighty God.

Acknowledgements:

First of all, we would like to thank God Almighty for His great love and continual work in our lives.

We are grateful to Keith, Seth, Mallory, and Isaac Pflum for sharing your wife and mom as the writer on our behalf.

We also thank Tami Pflum personally for giving so much of your time and effort in listening, praying, and typing.

We would like to thank Kent and Jan Heimer for sharing Cherry Valley with us for writing retreats and much-appreciated family bonding time.

Thanks to our counselor, Ron, and all the services provided at Apostolic Christian Counseling and Family Services.

And finally, we would like to thank the countless family and friends who knew of our book and prayed for God's blessings upon this endeavor.

Tom & Jolene Young

Note from the author....

Sitting down at the dining room table, I was immediately struck by something I noticed about the couple across from me. As he reached for her hand to begin our meeting in prayer, I observed an intimate connection that is missing from far too many marriages today. Not only their spoken words, but even the non-verbal communications I witnessed were evidence of a mutual love and respect freely flowing between them.

I was in their home to hear the testimony of a failed marriage, adultery, addiction, and eventually reconciliation, but before they'd even begun to share their story, I already found myself touched by the abundant manner in which our God had obviously healed and restored their broken relationship!

God has said in His word, "...I will restore to you the years that the locusts have eaten..." (Joel 2:25 KJV) I believe Tom & Jolene Young are living proof of that verse. When God chooses to enter into the restoration process, He doesn't merely return things to their original state. He often restores in such a way that far outshines the original. Consider Job. He lost almost everything. Very few of us can relate to the devastating losses he suffered in such a short time. Yet in the end, what did God do? We read in Job 42 that not only did the LORD restore Job's fortune; he increased all that he had twofold! Literally! Where before he had 7,000 sheep and 3,000 camels, 500 yoke of oxen and 500 female donkeys (Job 1:3) he ended up with exactly twice that amount: 14,000 sheep; 6,000 camels; 1,000 yoke of oxen and 1,000 female donkeys (Job 42:12). The LORD's restoration process is summarized simply, "Now the LORD blessed the latter days of Job more than his beginning…" (Job 42:12a). Talk about an understatement!

As you turn the pages of this book, it is my prayer that you will sense that same kind of blessing taking place in Tom and Jolene's lives. Believe me, this is the story of a God-sized restoration project! Christ alone is worthy of praise and glory for what He alone was capable of doing. Theirs is a story of much heartache and pain, but through it all God always had a plan. Sometimes, as humans, we make messes far beyond the scope of human repair. The Young's story is one of those situations. Only Jesus had the ability to pick up the broken pieces and rebuild them into the relationship they have today.

Although I have tried to maintain as much accuracy as possible in the retelling of Tom & Jolene's story, please understand I have taken some creative liberty in order to make it more enjoyable to the reader. However, the premise of the book and the healing power of Jesus Christ is 100% real. If you have lost hope today, whether because of a broken marriage, wayward child, financial setback, or any other reason, may you be encouraged by the story this book tells. And may you find comfort in knowing that it is in the situations where mortal eyes see only impossibilities that God has the opportunity to do some of His greatest work.

He is in the restoration business and is unsurpassed in what He does. It is a great privilege and honor to tell the great things He has done!

I will praise *You*, O LORD, with my whole heart; I will tell of all Your marvelous works. Psalms 9:1

Acknowledgements:

I *have been asked many times how I happened to write this book for the Youngs. Each time I revisit the journey, I once again stand in awe that an almighty God continually invites mere mortals to join Him in His work. It is humbling to know, although He doesn't truly need our help, He chooses to use humans to accomplish His mighty acts on earth! I am sharing parts of the journey here with the hope it will inspire each of you as much as it does me when I consider the way He worked to ensure this story was written.*

Several years ago I recognized one of my desires and life goals was to author a book of some sort. This desire lay dormant for quite awhile but, in spite of my lack of action, God was diligently at work behind the scenes. Completely unknown to me, in August 2010 my cousin Kent, who is also pastor / Elder of my church, shared my dream with an individual named Ted who was spending the weekend at his farm. When Ted returned to his workplace the following week, for whatever reason, he shared my desire with a coworker. I don't know exactly how that conversation went. But I do know that my Father was putting together a puzzle far more complex than any I would have envisioned!

That same week, Tom Young finally made a call to his counselor's office for advice. Although he had been hoping for over a year to have his and Jolene's true account published, he hadn't known where to begin the process of finding an author. But the Lord did! As only God could do, Tom was directed to Bill, the very coworker who surprisingly still held a seemingly useless piece of information tucked away in his brain from the conversation with Ted a few days prior. By that afternoon Tom left a voicemail asking if I would be interested in writing a book for him and his wife. And the rest, as they say, is history. My heartfelt gratitude goes to each individual who became an integral part of bringing this book into being. Thank you for allowing the Lord to use you to complete the puzzle!

Sharing with Ted definitely wasn't the last of Kent's involvement in this book. Words cannot express the deep gratitude in my heart to you and Jan for opening your cabin for our annual writing retreats. Thank you both for believing in this project from the start and always being faithful encouragers, servant-leaders, and beautiful examples of what it means to live for Jesus! I am most grateful for your willingness to pray over the manuscript, believing in faith God has plans to work mightily through this book. We may never know until Heaven how many lives will be touched and changed because of the intercessory prayer offered as a group that night at your cabin. Thank you for the laying on of hands and anointing this work. I hope the memory of that prayer will never be forgotten by any who were in attendance!

Rick, Kim, Clayton, Jordan, Trevin and Shalise...thanks for being a part of our retreats, providing comic relief when we were bogged down in editing for too many hours, helping with food prep, and simply making memories with us. You have become like family and I am so blessed that God allowed our life journeys to cross. Life would be much lonelier without all of you!

Megan, thanks for your accountability over the years, beginning with that long-ago challenge regarding life goals and spiritual gifts. Along the way you've inspired me to a deeper awareness of our Abba Father constantly weaving the pages of life into a plot much more complex than anything we could imagine or dream! Oh, and although I didn't quite meet the goal of a published book by age 40, at least I'm within the right decade!

Brent & Charlotte, I'll never forget that monetary gift you blessed me with as I made the first trip to interview the Youngs. You didn't only provide gas money; you provided support and love in a tangible way that meant so much and have remained faithful encouragers throughout the process. Thank you!

For all of those who knew my desire and love of writing and have encouraged me in various ways to use this passion for God's glory, I thank you! I hesitate to list names because there are so many of you who consistently prayed, checked in, commented on

Instagram and Facebook, or supported this project in some other way. You know who you are, especially a certain someone who took on so much ownership in the project she actually started calling it "her" book! I have been abundantly blessed with an amazing circle of prayer warriors and thank each of you from the bottom of my heart for storming Heaven's gates on my behalf! This book has a message of hope that Satan obviously doesn't want told. There were plenty of days in the writing process when he came hard at me. Thank you for your prayer cover on those days...and for all the prayers you prayed for the individuals and couples who may eventually read this book.

I offer a heartfelt thanks to each one in the Grimm and Pflum family who have consistently prayed for and encouraged me throughout life and especially through this project! I was incredibly blessed to be born into one family and marry into the other. I truly love each one of you!

Jeanne, you might not have wanted a baby sister your senior year, but you have become my biggest cheerleader and you definitely deserve a special shout out! I can't thank you enough for opening your home for Jolene and me to meet early on in this process, for entertaining and feeding all our kids that day, providing a quiet setting for me to work on my book on multiple occasions, and for always believing in me no matter what. Bill, your feedback on the rough draft meant more than you will ever know!

Don, I appreciate the hours you stayed with Dad so I could write. You're the best brother in the world, hands down. And Tricia, thanks for all the times you let the kids play and eat at your house so I could continue writing uninterrupted. We can't pick our relatives but if I had to pick anyone to be doubly related to, it would be you two!

Those carefree days of playwriting and acting seem like a lifetime ago in some ways and a blink of the eye in others, Renee'. Oh, how life has had its share of twists and turns since then. Thank you for being a daily inspiration to me as you press onward, daily clinging to Christ as your All-in-All. The refiner's fire has done a mighty work in you. Thanks for praying and be assured I pray for you in return.

Mumsie Dear, all my life you beautifully modeled how to use the gift of writing for God's glory and the good of others. The countless letters of encouragement you have written throughout the years have made a difference in untold lives. I am honored God chose to bless me with the gift of writing, also, and only pray that I will "occupy the talent until He returns" as faithfully as you have!

I am forever grateful to you, Dad, for speaking my love language so clearly. Thank you for being full of affirmation for me but even more importantly for mom. Because of the way you loved her, our home was a secure haven from the world. Being able to care for you in this season of your life is a blessing and such a small way to pay you back for all you have done for me throughout my life.

Seth, Mallory and Isaac, I'm so honored to be called "Mom" by you three God-given blessings! Being a mom is literally the hardest thing I've ever done, but without a doubt the most rewarding. Thank you for understanding when I kept writing through suppertime and you were stuck eating leftovers (again). Our heart-to-heart chats are some of the highlights of my life so I'm sorry for the times throughout this project when I was distracted or preoccupied and missed an opportunity for conversation. All three of you have taught me about forgiveness and unconditional love. I have enjoyed watching each of you growing and maturing into the unique individuals God created you to be and can't wait to watch the rest of your lives unfold. Remember to always let your Creator write your stories for you. He's the best author in the Universe, hands down, and His storyline is above and beyond anything any of us could or would imagine!

Keith, my husband, lover, friend; to you I owe an incredible amount! Thank you for recognizing this book project as my "Mt. Rainier" early on and standing behind me, supporting me throughout the lengthy journey. You never complained about the amount of time I sat staring at the computer as household messes piled up around me. I appreciate more than you know every single dish you washed, each time you cared for Dad in my place, took kids somewhere to give me some peace and quiet, or graciously encouraged me to leave everything and get away on a Saturday to write. I am so grateful God gave me you. Thanks for being my practical, steady rock and protector. I am beyond thankful for the way Jesus wrote our love story and look forward to growing old at your side.

Shelby, Shania and Shayna, you have amazing parents...and you are amazing daughters! Thanks for all the encouraging comments you sent my way, for being excited about this project, and just for being yourselves! Observing the three of you running hard after Jesus is a living testimony to what Christ can do! He took the brokenness in your family and redeemed it, creating one of the most beautiful, love-filled families I know!

Tom and Jolene, I am deeply grateful to you for blessing me with the honor and privilege of writing this book. Thank you for entrusting your story to me and for being patient as it drug out much longer than any of us ever imagined it would. Thanks for always being transparent and real as you allowed glimpses into your personal lives. Jo, the permission to read your private journals was humbling and also invaluable as it helped me get to know you so much better. When I think of the five of you, I truly praise God for the way He intertwined our families, showering not only us, but also our children, with friendships that will last an eternity!

Last of all, I could never have accomplished this task without the unending grace of God. I give Him all glory and honor for gifting me with a passion for writing. It is my deepest desire He will take my human effort in writing this story and work miracles of God-sized proportion, restoring marriages and bringing prodigal spouses home. If just one marriage is restored or spared from divorce, the many hours spent at my computer will definitely have been worth it all!

Tami Pflum

Introduction:

*F*ew couples truly grasp the significance of the commitment being made on their wedding day when they stand and take turns saying, "I do". There are most likely only a pessimistic few who envision a life of poverty, hardship, betrayal, disease, loneliness, or handicap in that moment.

The rest of us eagerly pledge to love and cherish one another, "In good times, in bad, during sickness and health, until death do we part," without really considering the depth of what we are promising.

Yet God sometimes allows us to experience obstacles or hardships that put our commitment to the test. In those moments we are faced with a very personal and potentially life-altering decision: Were our vows merely empty words or are we truly willing to live them out, regardless of the cost?

One difficult question often leads to another. Does God really expect us to keep the promises we made, no matter what the circumstances? Or are there exceptions to our commitment; loopholes and "escape clauses" in our vows?

Consider the young attorney and his wife who had a bright future ahead of them following a cross-country move to practice in a thriving community on the east coast. Months later, a debilitating stroke robbed her of her ability to function normally or even communicate with her husband. Now faced with an uncertain future of daily visits with his invalid, unresponsive wife in a nursing home, he wonders how long he can endure. Some days he allows himself to dream of being free to love someone who can return his love.

Or the soldier struck by a landmine while defending his country. Remaining married to a double amputee whose personality has drastically changed for the worse is far from the storybook ending his wife imagined on their wedding day. Is she expected to stay the course?

What about the man who suddenly discovers his spouse of twenty years has been living a lie? Drifting from one affair to another throughout the span of their marriage, she has broken their vows repeatedly. Is it fair to ask him to remain faithful when she obviously hasn't?

As Christians, we may find it easy to spout off quick, black-and-white answers to hypothetical questions like these...but if asked to walk in the shoes of any individual mentioned here, would our answers suddenly become shrouded in shades of gray? What would you do if your spouse had been unfaithful? Would you choose to hold fast to your vows, knowing full well you may be opening yourself up to further pain, deceit, heartache, or loneliness? Or would you deliberately label yourself the victim, thereby justifying the decision to walk away from the promises made?

Based on the typical vows, there are no caveats; no disclaimers only holding us responsible to love and cherish on the days that our spouse seems lovable or worth cherishing. Instead, marriage requires a day-to-day, moment-by-moment commitment to place our spouse's needs above our own...to love as Christ calls us to. In fact, we are called to a love like His.

This, for many, proves too great a task.

Please understand this book is not meant to address every issue or apply to every situation. There are certainly cases of abuse— both physical as well as emotional—when, for the safety of the victim, separation may be the best and only solution. It is not my intent whatsoever to add any guilt to the already heavy burden laid upon someone in that kind of situation.

But outside of those circumstances, isn't it God's desire that what He what He has joined together man does not tear apart?

Tom and Jolene were faced with many complex questions. Instead of casting judgment upon the choices made, may we each be challenged to inspect our own lives, honestly assessing if we are upholding our own vows, or if there are areas of our life we are holding onto instead of relinquishing all to our Savior and allowing His Sovereign will to be accomplished in and through us. It is important to remember He may not always choose to work in the same manner in which He did for the Youngs, but He does promise to sustain and pour out daily grace upon those who trust in Him!

Reconcilable Differences
The True Story of Tom and Jolene Young
Written by Tami Pflum

Chapter 1

—◆✖◆—

Waking with a sense of expectation, Jolene Young glanced around the bedroom she'd shared the past five years with her husband, Tom. Not one to embrace change easily, she was surprised at the excitement she felt this morning. Just yesterday they had accepted an offer on the sale of their house and soon the process of packing would begin.

Although Jolene had experienced mixed emotions when Tom first suggested placing their house on the market, after prayerfully seeking direction from God she was confident she was obeying not only her husband but also her Lord in this decision.

Following months of disillusionment and hurt, she was unfamiliar with the small seedling of hope taking root in her heart. She felt some of the tension of the past few months lift ever so slightly as she anticipated moving to a new town and a fresh start with Tom and their three young girls.

Little did she know that very soon the hope which was just beginning to bud in her soul was going to be trampled under the feet of one who had vowed to love and cherish her as long as they both should live.

Hearing muffled voices coming from the kitchen, Jolene realized their two older daughters were waiting on her for breakfast. She quietly slipped out of bed and tiptoed from the room, being careful not to disturb her sleeping husband. Currently working nights at a corporate office, Tom had only been home a few hours and would likely remain in bed until midmorning.

Although she'd been scheduled to work at the local meat locker today, her plans had changed the evening before when Tom called during his break and asked her to take the day off. Uncertain why he would make such an unusual request, she'd hesitated before questioning, "Is this a good thing?"

His immediate and cheerful reply had caught her off guard. "Absolutely!"

As she'd hung up from the unusual call, for a brief moment she'd allowed herself to consider what he had up his sleeve. An unexpected flicker of anticipation had coursed through her body before she'd quickly stifled it. By the time she'd cleaned up the kitchen and folded some laundry, all thoughts of the next day had been pushed aside.

But now, with the September sun pouring in through the window, Jolene sensed a warm ray of some unnamed emotion beginning to penetrate the cold recesses of her heart. She went to greet Shelby and Shania with more enthusiasm than she'd felt in quite awhile.

In spite of her care not to bother Tom, he had heard Jolene leave the room and was now lying awake in bed with his mind racing. Hoping to get more sleep, he rolled over and threw his arm over his eyes to block out the morning light seeping through the blinds.

After a few restless moments, Tom gave up on any more sleep as his mind replayed the events of the last few days.

He was amazed how quickly his plans seemed to be falling into place. Admittedly, he had anticipated more of a battle from Jolene when he first suggested putting their home up for sale and moving to the nearby city of Bloomington, in which he worked. He had made sure to point out how logical it would be; moving would save him an hour commute each way to his job. Still, his initial attempts to convince her had seemed to fall on deaf ears. So he had been rather surprised when, within a relatively short time, she agreed to list the house without any further struggle.

He'd been even more surprised six days later when they had received a signed offer!

Contemplating the path life was taking, he was undecided what label to give his emotions. Excitement? Apprehension?

Tom was almost afraid to peel the layers back too far, instinctively aware he might uncover regret if he dug deep enough. Hearing Jolene stirring around the kitchen, he rehearsed how he would break the news to her later that day.

When Tom finally emerged from the bedroom and suggested she take the girls to his parents' so they could be alone, Jolene found herself encouraged by his body language. She noticed the way he made eye contact and even smiled at her. How long had it been since she'd been warmed by his smile; since she'd felt like he was not only looking *at* her, but actually *seeing* her?

In light of the recent events in their relationship, she'd learned to protect her feelings by shutting off her emotions. But she sensed something different in his interaction today. Did she dare give in, even a little, to the blossoming hope?

While Tom grabbed a bite to eat, Jolene gathered a diaper bag for eleven month old Shayna and headed out the door with all three girls, grateful for her in-laws' willingness to watch them at a moment's notice. Her mind raced during the short drive, once again trying to imagine what her husband might have planned. Relying on his assurance it was something positive, her thoughts ran wild with possibilities, in spite of trying to keep her imagination in check.

Upon her return home, she found Tom still in the kitchen, nursing a cup of coffee. Wordlessly, she followed him as he moved to the door and out into the backyard. Instinctively, they made their way to the swing set.

There, soaking up the warm rays of sunshine on that gorgeous fall morning, both were inwardly filled with anticipation regarding the days to come. While Jolene desperately hoped for renewal in their marriage, little did she know Tom's thoughts and actions were being driven by his burning desire for freedom from all that he viewed "stifling".

Once they were situated, Tom wasted no time getting to the point. "After we close on the house, I want to separate, Jolene. I need to find myself, so I plan to rent an apartment in Bloomington." Pausing only long enough to draw in a short breath, he continued in a rush, "You and the girls can go anywhere you want; just not next door to me."

The harsh words sliced through her like a dagger as the reality of what he'd just said began to sink in. She felt fingers of fear taking root and squeezing the life out of the tiny seedling of hope in her heart.

Trying to process what he meant, an overwhelming vulnerability clamped down upon her. As of this morning they'd accepted an offer for their home. He'd led her to believe they would be starting afresh by moving to Bloomington together, as a family. This was supposed to be their "second chance". Now, without a house, where was she to go? How could she provide for their three little girls without him?

Somehow, with a will of their own, her legs continued to pump the swing while a multitude of questions swirled in her mind. How had life gotten this far off track from everything she had once envisioned? They were supposed to be Christians: Christ-followers. They had sought Christ's direction for their marriage from the very beginning!

Before their wedding, she had fully expected to share a thriving, healthy relationship with Tom. But along the way life had taken so many unexpected turns it was hardly recognizable as the dream she'd once imagined. At least that's how it had seemed.

Until this morning.

When she woke today, in a house they were in the process of selling in order to begin paying off their mounting bills, she'd had the impression better days were just around the corner for them. She'd believed Tom was finally ready to focus on repairing a marriage that had been bruised severely over the years. She'd even dared to hope they'd eventually find their way back to their original dreams.

So had she really heard correctly? How could he want to separate now? Confusion muddled her thoughts as her brain tried to rationalize what he truly meant. Hadn't Tom said his reason for wanting to talk to her today was a good thing? What about this was good? Perhaps she was missing something. Or maybe she truly had misunderstood.

But the words replayed in her mind once again. "...I want to separate, Jolene...You and the girls can go anywhere you want; just not next door to me."

Still trying to process what had just happened, tears began to flow as one emotion after another slammed into her. Her feelings swung wildly between hurt, confusion, anger, and finally embarrassment as she realized how he had tricked her into going along with his plan to sell the house. He'd even manipulated her into taking time off work today for this conversation to take place.

Bringing the swing to an abrupt stop, Jolene began repeatedly kicking both feet against the grass in sudden anger at the thought of being deceived like she had. "I should have known! How could I not have known what you were up to?" Her anger seemed to be directed more at herself than towards Tom, as if she couldn't bear the thought of having overlooked the obvious. No one had supported her in the decision to sell the house. Now, realizing everyone else had been right after all, she felt all the more foolish.

In spite of the warm sunshine, she shivered as she sensed the newborn glimmer in her heart being extinguished.

In her spirit she cried out to the only One left to turn to as the pieces of her life were shattering all around her. *"What now, God?"*

She heard only silence in return.

Where was God in all of this? How had He allowed this to happen? *Why* had He allowed it to happen?

Like Jolene, have you ever felt your hope dashed into pieces and ground into the dust? If so, you need to ask yourself in whom (or what) is your hope placed. If your hope is in anyone or anything other than Christ you are in a vulnerable position. Plans will *change. Dreams* will *be dashed. Health* will *fail. Loved ones* will *let you down. The question is, when hope crumbles, how will you react? Will you turn against or blame God for allowing—or even causing—the pain? Or will you turn to Him in confidence, placing your trust in His love and fully believing that whatever He allows to come into your life is truly for the best?*

Where is your hope today? Is it firmly planted in the unshakable promises of God and His faithfulness? Don't settle for anything less!

Chapter 2

$\mathcal{I}$n the days that followed, Tom seemed strangely detached, going about his daily routine with some semblance of normalcy. On the other hand, Jolene only mustered the strength to get out of bed each morning for the sake of Shelby, Shania, and Shayna. She somehow managed to put on a brave front for the girls, in spite of the numbness which had taken up residency in the corner of her heart left vacant after hope moved out.

Almost hourly she'd find herself considering what had gone wrong to bring them to this point in their marriage.

She knew the adage well, "It takes two to tango." However, considering the issues that had dogged them from the beginning of their relationship, the percentage of responsibility she felt she had to own up to was extremely small in comparison to the percentage of blame she credited to Tom's account.

With Tom still in bed and the girls waiting on breakfast, Jolene began assembling the ingredients she'd need for one of her favorite dishes. Having made egg cups countless times before, she went through the motions without needing to focus on the task at hand. Instead, her mind drifted back through the years.

Although she couldn't recall the first time she'd met Tom, it felt like they'd always known one another in spite of growing up in different communities. Because they shared a mutual aunt and uncle, they'd seen one another at various family events over the years, as well as church functions within the denomination to which both their families belonged. In fact, Tom and Jolene had been acquaintances—friends, even—as far back as she could remember.

The third of five children in a close-knit family, Jolene Schambach had grown up in a western suburb of Chicago. As she cracked eggs into each little cup, her mind went back through the years to her high school days when Tommy Young had surrendered his life to Christ. His choice to become a part of the Apostolic Christian church was a serious commitment, one which meant a radical change of lifestyle, and one which she had not yet been willing to make.

In spite of being a minister's daughter, in a family whose social life primarily centered on church activities, Jolene had resisted her Savior throughout her school years. After graduating from high school she'd chosen to remain at home and attend Elgin Community College, pursuing a degree in elementary education on a softball scholarship.

Reflecting back on that period of her life, she distinctly remembered even then having a strange sense she would one day marry Tom.

Carefully sliding the egg cups into the oven and setting the timer, Jolene allowed herself a few more moments of dwelling on the past, in spite of a daunting to-do list demanding her attention.

She recalled, as if it had been yesterday, the emotional day her own life had changed forever.

Even as a young child Jolene had understood the plan of salvation and her need of repentance, but over the years she had learned to drown out the Lord's voice whenever she sensed Him tenderly calling out to her. She always told herself, "Someday" she would answer His pleading invitation. "Someday" finally arrived during her first semester in college. Finding she could no longer resist Jesus, she had surrendered her heart and soul to His saving grace and power on September 30, 1995.

Not once had she regretted that decision. Even now, as the pain in her heart at times grew so intense it seemed as if it would suffocate her, she knew it was only because of God's sustaining grace she was able to continue putting one foot in front of the other. Surrendering her heart to her Savior had definitely been the best decision she'd ever made.

Becoming a new creation in Christ, she had turned her back on the old Jolene. The weekend of March 2, 1996 she had shared her testimony of faith in Jesus with her church family and publicly declared her commitment to Christ through baptism.

Along with her new life in Christ, Jolene had begun facing a new struggle in her feelings towards Tom. Suddenly she'd found herself desiring to see him more and more often, hoping their paths would cross so she would have opportunity to talk to him. At the same time she wasn't sure how her attention would be perceived by him or others and definitely didn't want to put her own feelings ahead of God's direction for her life.

So she did her best to put thoughts of Tom aside. Yet in spite of her best attempts, as Jolene tried to concentrate on her college coursework or study for an exam, there were times she was completely consumed with thoughts of Tom. Exasperated by the struggle, she finally resorted to pleading with God to remove any feelings that weren't from Him.

During that time, her brother had become engaged and the family was thrust into the craziness of planning a wedding within a few short months. Jolene clearly remembered the conflicting emotions that had warred within her. Close to her brother, she rejoiced with him and his fiancée, but inside her heart the longing to be in their shoes had intensified. She'd wondered when *her* turn would come and if Tom would be the one for her.

When her brother's wedding day arrived Jolene had found herself secretly hoping Tom would be in attendance. Even if she didn't get to talk to him, at least she'd catch a glimpse of the face that filled her thoughts so often.

Little did she know how quickly her life was about to change!

Unknown to Jolene at the time, Tom had been facing struggles of his own in regards to her. He had later informed her he couldn't help but be drawn to her carefree and somewhat flirtatious personality. Deep down he'd desired to be married but sometimes felt guilty for even having the desire. Not wanting to ever be accused of not serving the Lord wholeheartedly, he had been concerned that longing for marriage somehow meant he wasn't single-minded enough. So throughout the years, when their paths crossed, he had attempted to convince himself he felt nothing for Jolene Schambach. However, it seemed like every time he turned around, there she'd been!

Sometimes he had the distinct feeling God was intentionally laying her on his heart and mind for a reason. He just didn't want to misinterpret the message.

One weekend their mutual cousin from Ohio invited him and his youth group for a visit. Attempting to be low key, Tom had casually asked if Jolene's church was invited. He wasn't entirely sure if he wanted the answer to be "Yes" or "No". When he was told they were not coming, he found himself somewhat relieved. In all honesty, at times he grew weary of the struggles it brought on each time his and Jolene's paths crossed.

In light of his sleuthing ahead of time, he couldn't have been more surprised that Saturday evening when he arrived at the church function and heard someone off-handedly mention that the Elgin, Illinois youth group had been invited after all. This person went on to specifically mention Jolene as one of those planning to be in attendance. Immediately Tom felt his heart rate double. Extremely nervous all of a sudden he realized he definitely could not deny that the prospect of seeing Jolene had a huge impact on him!

Over the next two weeks not a night passed without Tom dreaming about Jolene and marriage. One dream in particular had been so vivid and realistic he couldn't shake it even after waking. In his dream he heard someone announce that Tom Young was getting married. However, the speaker didn't say to whom. Instead, a line of women began filing past Tom, one by one. As each one passed, he heard his own voice declare, "No!" Suddenly Jolene appeared in the line. As she confidently strolled by, he heard himself give a resounding and enthusiastic, "Yes!"

Soon after, Tom taught a Sunday School class in which the focus was mainly on Joseph's dreams coming true in Genesis. He began to wonder if there had been meaning in his own dreams and if he needed to pay attention to whatever message the Lord was trying to convey.

Finally Tom began to earnestly seek answers from God regarding his future and the possibility of marriage to Jolene. Within a short time he had gone to his pastor and shared his intent of asking for Jolene's hand in marriage.

Rather than basing her marriage on her own feelings or infatuation, Jolene had always known she wanted to depend on the Spirit's direction when it came time to find a lifelong mate. Growing up in a church that practiced faith marriages rather than dating, Jolene was aware those looking in from the outside had plenty of questions about the process. Several times she had even heard her church falsely accused of practicing arranged marriages for the members.

When Jolene received the proposal of marriage to Tom she came to a startling realization. Suddenly she saw it with greater clarity; their marriages actually *were* arranged! It just happened to be far different than the manner assumed by many. Instead of parents or church leadership choosing a mate for an individual, *God* was allowed to arrange the marriage. And who could be better suited to play "Holy Matchmaker" than the Creator of the two individuals He chose to join?

In her heart, Jolene had immediately sensed the answer would be "Yes" based on all the feelings she already had for Tom. But before giving a reply, she'd wanted sufficient time to allow God to direct her future and plainly prove His will to her. She strongly desired the security and reassurance of a spouse chosen for her by God, rather than her own emotions.

Over the course of the next few days she had spent more time than usual in prayer and pouring over God's Word, carrying her Bible with her to work so she could seek answers from the Lord during any lulls between customers. Jolene found great comfort in various Scriptures she read throughout the week and was amazed at the blanket of peace that surrounded her whenever she considered marrying Tom. The sense of peace had been palpable enough that a friend had asked her what was going on in her life to make her so calm all the sudden. It was evident to Jolene that God was speaking to her in the midst of her searching.

In addition to overwhelming peace regarding Tom's proposal, one night Jolene had read two phrases in 2 Kings 5 that spoke directly to her heart. "Go in peace" and "All is well". Like a comforting nudge, they gave her courage and confidence she was to take this step of faith and join her heart and life to Tom.

They had eventually announced their engagement on November 10, 1996.

Thinking back to that time of seeking direction from God, Jolene was so thankful she had waited on the Lord for His assurance and approval. With her marriage now unraveling, she still could return to that time and remember how God had clearly directed her heart and given her an incredibly deep peace that marrying Tom was within the pastureland of His will and plan for her life. No matter what the future held for them from this point forward, she still clung to the assurance their marriage had not been a mistake in God's eyes!

As the buzz of the kitchen timer briefly snapped her back to reality, Jolene was struck by a bizarre realization: in spite of her pleading with God to remove her feelings prior to the proposal, they had firmly remained.

Until sometime during their brief engagement.

By this time her oldest brother had also become engaged and was married in early December. The weekend of his wedding there were already rising doubts in her relationship with Tom. With him in town for a couple of days, Jolene had been blindsided by her lack of feelings. Bombarded by conflicting emotions, she remembered most unnerving of all was the thought that weekend she'd cared more for Tom *before* they'd been engaged than she did *after*.

The irony of that realization from years ago stuck with her as she called the girls to breakfast.

Putting on a cheerful smile for her daughters, she found herself wondering if Tom's thoughts ever drifted back in time the way hers frequently did.

If so, maybe somehow, some way, they would find the road back to where life had gotten so miserably off track and chart a new path for their future; the one God had intended for them all along.

Chapter 3

*A*s Jolene reminisced in the kitchen that morning, Tom was just waking. Also in a pensive mood, he allowed himself to focus on days gone by more than he had in a long, long time. Whenever he thought back to the hopes and dreams he'd once had for his life, his current situation suddenly seemed distasteful.

Conviction was unsettling. He'd rather just forget the past and push forward to whatever the future held.

But for some reason he couldn't shake off the memories today, so puffing his pillow up under his head, he rolled to his back. Staring at the ceiling, scenes from the past came clearly into focus in his mind.

He saw himself at thirteen years old, a pack of cigarettes hidden in his pocket. At the time he hadn't wanted to dwell on the disappointment it would bring to his parents if they knew what he was hiding. Not only them; most of the neighbors were from his church or a similar conservative denomination and he didn't want any of them to know he'd developed a smoking habit at such a young age.

Throughout that summer he occasionally snuck off to the barn to smoke in secret, but primarily kept his unhealthy habit confined to the hours he spent working on a detasseling crew. There, far from the eyes of those who might care, he had often lit up during break times, relishing the feeling of fitting in with the other smokers on the crew.

Somewhere along the way he had begun to ask himself why it mattered if his family and others saw him for who he really was. Why was he so concerned what others thought? The more he'd mulled that question over, the more he'd come to realize it was because he longed to be identified with those very people. He'd wanted what they had; the stability that came from belonging. In this case, belonging to a church family. Yes, deep down he knew he wanted to eventually join the Apostolic Christian Church and live the kind of life his parents did; a life free from addictive habits like smoking.

With the realization came a sense of shame, knowing his actions would deeply disappoint the very ones he wanted to someday be like. The more thought he'd given it, the more he realized how tired he was of the way he was living. He was sick of hiding the cigarettes, sick of his miserable existence and the frightening sense that he was going to get sucked deeper and deeper into a life of sin if he didn't escape it now. Most of all, he was tired of fearing hell. Many nights he worried he would die a sinner and end up spending an eternity in torment and regret.

Finally, on November 12, 1988 Tom gave his dad an incredible birthday gift with the news he was done running from God and wanted to begin a new life.

It had been a new beginning in his life, for sure. Soon he had replaced old friendships, habits, and passions with new ones. He had thrown himself into church life wholeheartedly, fully embracing the traditions and expectations placed on him. Whenever niggling doubts that something was amiss tried to creep into his mind, he had learned how to push them away by keeping busy.

Tom was a "doer".

Very sociable, he had thrived on attending his church's youth activities. In fact, his devoted involvement had led to his being elected as an "officer" in his youth group.

Always willing to plan an activity, he'd also walked a delicate line of trying to please others, carefully avoiding anything that might upset someone he respected.

He hadn't ever wanted to admit to anyone, not even himself, but he often grew weary of trying to please everyone. Some days he had practically run himself ragged in the process. In spite of his best efforts he had definitely found the saying, "You can please some of the people all of the time and all of the people some of the time, but you can't please all of the people all of the time" to be full of truth. Yet that hadn't stopped him from trying. If only he had understood that attempting to please everyone fails to please the Lord. Even God fails to please all the people all the time and He never asks the impossible of His people.

The voices of his daughters outside his bedroom snapped his mind to the present, but only momentarily.

Soon he was reliving the past again.

Tom had been thrilled when Jolene had agreed to his marriage proposal. With great anticipation, he'd fully expected their engagement to bring deep satisfaction.

Unfortunately, it hadn't. Quite the opposite, really. He recalled how his initial excitement had been replaced with anxiousness early on in their engagement. As his doubts and worries had increased, a friend had even encouraged him to call off the upcoming wedding. But Tom had been determined. His firm reply had been, "I've been shown by God this is what I'm supposed to do, so I am going to make it work!"

Obviously he had failed to do so. He hadn't dared to admit until recently his marriage to Jolene had definitely left him yearning for something more. Though they'd occasionally shared moments of happiness, from his perspective the negatives far out-weighed the positives.

Suddenly, he had been face to face with an emptiness he'd never felt, or at least never acknowledged, before. He sensed a longing for something that his heart had never found. But what was it?

In his days as a young believer, Tom had read the Word and prayed regularly. But as time wore on his Christianity had taken on more "religion" and less "relationship". Consumed more and more with the expectations of others, he found less and less joy in serving the Lord. He came to view church and his spiritual life as little more than one restriction after another.

Whenever he'd tried to explain his feelings to Jolene they inevitably ended up arguing. It sometimes seemed like she, too, was aggravated by restrictions; it just seemed to be a different set than those which bothered him. Why was it they usually seemed worlds apart in their perspective and communication?

Eventually, his desire to be understood contributed to him crossing lines he'd never imagined he would cross. In his mind it had started out innocently. All he'd wanted was someone to hear him out. He had found a listening ear in a co-worker who was going through rough times in her own marriage. With each conversation he had let his guard down a little more...until he had found himself emotionally attached to a woman who was not his wife.

Without realizing it or, perhaps more honestly, without choosing to recognize it, the attraction had become physical.

Until one day the unthinkable had happened. Although he had not necessarily set out to be unfaithful, he had knowingly placed himself in a risky relationship and then allowed himself to ride the waves of emotion and passion rather than actively fleeing from what he knew to be wrong.

In the nights leading up to his downfall he'd gotten a taste of the headiness which freedom from restrictions and responsibilities brought with it. As he'd stayed out until three or four in the morning, doing what he *wanted* to do instead of what he thought he *should* do, he was exhilarated by an excitement beyond anything he had ever experienced before.

Even now the headiness called and beckoned, whispering that what his heart longed for was liberty from everyone and everything he once claimed to hold dear: his family, his church, his God.

It seemed he had found what Proverbs 9:17 speaks of, "Stolen water is sweet, and bread eaten in secret is pleasant." Unfortunately, he didn't realize how true the next verse also is: "But he does not know that the dead are there, that her guests *are* in the depths of hell." At this point Satan had so thoroughly deceived him, Tom wasn't aware what a slippery slope he was heading down.

———— ❄ ————

As Tom dropped his feet to the floor he reached for the pack of cigarettes he'd purchased on the way home from work earlier that morning. He knew Jolene hated it when he smoked, but what did that matter anymore? He was free to do whatever he wanted since they would be heading separate ways very soon.

Making his way towards the backyard to light up, Tom once again considered how his rocky marriage had only served to magnify the barrenness in his life. It stood to reason, then, that being released from responsibility to everyone and everything that felt like a ball and chain around his neck would finally fill the gaping void in his heart.

Little did he know he was simply digging himself a deeper hole.

"There is a God-shaped vacuum in the heart of every man which cannot be filled by any created thing, but only by God, the Creator, made known through Jesus." It is debated whether the above quote was truly penned by French philosopher Blaise Pascal or, more likely, a paraphrase of his original words, but regardless of where it originated, the meaning is profound.

Consider what these words convey about the nature of our loving, merciful Father: Out of great compassion for the human race God provided His own blameless Son as an offering for a sin debt that couldn't be paid. But then He went a step further and created within each and every soul a yearning for Himself in order that we would seek—and find—salvation! Without a doubt it is

His desire that everyone would come to know Him personally: "Who desires all men to be saved and to come to the knowledge of the truth." (1 Tim. 2:4)

Isn't it true that every one of us at one time or another have longed for something more, some deeper purpose in life? Yet, while most of us will acknowledge—either consciously or subconsciously—the vacuum which exists in our innermost being, too few ever come to understand the only means by which the void can be filled is by allowing the One who placed it there to come and live within us. Instead, many frantically search to fill the hollowness in their life in every way imaginable, only to be repeatedly disappointed. While some may seek pleasure, power, or perfection in an imperfect world, others fill the empty places with family, friends, a job, even church activities or good works. Unfortunately, just because those things are "good" doesn't mean they are sufficient. None should ever take the rightful place of Christ in anyone's life. To allow them to do so is to allow the simplest form of idolatry into one's heart.

Our loving Creator designed us with an instinctual need to be filled with Him, and Him alone. Because our hearts were created for worship, we will each end up worshipping something or someone, intentionally or unintentionally. The question is, "Who will it be?"

Pause and take time to answer this question: who, or what, are you worshipping today? Anything less than Jesus will leave you empty and purposeless, continually longing for more. Worst of all, Satan may not only be blinding you to the source of the vacuum in your life, he may even completely blind you to its existence. Just like Tom.

Chapter 4

*C*risp days and cool nights brought magnificent color to the trees as September marched on. By now, their plans to separate were known to many, including their family.

While preparing for Shayna's 1st birthday party, Jolene emotionally steeled herself for the all-too-familiar charade she knew she would be forced to play once the guests began to arrive. Expecting both sides of the family, she was well aware there were bound to be uncomfortable moments ahead for everyone.

After busying herself with finishing touches on the table, she glanced out the window to see if anyone had pulled in the driveway. With no cars yet in sight, her attention shifted to the landscape. She couldn't help but sense a parallel to her own life as she noticed the swirling autumn breeze stripping brilliant leaves from the trees, carelessly scattering them on the ground.

When she and Tom had first been engaged life had held promise and beauty, just like the radiant leaves outside. It had been easy to imagine days of golden sunshine and bright hope for their future.

But it hadn't been long before storm clouds were beginning to brew on the horizon. Even before their wedding day, strong winds of doubt had blown against their relationship.

At first, the biggest struggle for Jolene had been moving away from Elgin. As the excitement of being engaged had worn off and reality set in, she'd begun questioning everything. Yet deep down she'd still believed God had opened this door and was the One leading her down this path. She just didn't understand why it had to be so hard if it was part of God's plan.

On the other hand, Tom had initially seemed happy and as if everything was going well. But as the engagement wore on, with Jolene's concerns and questions becoming more and more noticeable, he'd begun to experience his own doubts. She had watched in surprise as he'd been transformed in a relatively short period of time from a confident, secure leader in the youth group to an anxious and insecure fiancé. What bothered her the most was not having a clue what had happened to so completely alter his personality.

Following a huge snowstorm the week prior, the morning of their wedding had dawned beautiful, sunny, and warm for February. Looking back on that day, Jolene clearly remembered how she had felt as she'd waited to walk down the aisle. Extremely nauseous, she had gone so far as to ask her maid of honor why she felt like this and if she should really go through with the wedding or call it off right then and there. It had taken all her strength to muster the courage needed to walk towards the front of the church, meet Tom, and eventually stand with him to take her vows.

Following the service was a buffet reception. As it drew to a close Jolene had drug her feet, not wanting to leave, as if procrastinating would keep the inevitable goodbyes from happening. The idea of moving away from her own family and church was almost more than she could bear at the time.

Next she recalled one of their first major confrontations in marriage. Only two months after the wedding, Jolene had been feeling particularly homesick, missing family and friends. Moving away and adjusting to a new home, church and job, as well as small town living versus life in the Chicago suburbs had all proven much more difficult than she'd anticipated.

And then there was her brand new role as wife to become accustomed to.

So Jolene had been grateful when she and Tom received an invitation from a young couple close to their age who had only been married a few years. She was hoping an evening with peers would help ease her loneliness and perhaps provide the beginning of a new friendship in the community.

As they made the short drive that afternoon, Jolene decided to take advantage of the time alone in the car to discuss her plans to make a trip back to Elgin to visit family.

However, she'd been startled by Tom's reaction to her request to go home. He'd responded with a quick and unyielding, "No!" When she pushed the issue, he abruptly reminded her she'd just been home a couple weeks before and he felt there was no reason to make the trip again so soon. Frustrated by his lack of understanding, she tried to make him see it from her perspective.

"*I'm* the one who had to move away from *my* family; you didn't! I'm with *you* six days a week. Why can't I go back to Elgin once in a while to see everyone? Why don't you ever care how I feel?"

The accusing words had hung between them for several long seconds while Tom's rising anger became evident. With jaw muscle tensed, his knuckles whitened as he gripped the steering wheel tighter.

For the next few minutes they had vacillated between stony silences and heated arguing. At one point, Tom had gone so far as to remind her that his own grandmother had moved across the country, all the way from Connecticut to Illinois, and *she'd* managed just fine without going home to see *her* family all the time!

A sense of alarm had coursed through Jolene. What was happening to them? They were newlyweds, for goodness sake! People would still expect them to be in the infatuation stage of early love; instead they were so upset they were yelling and carelessly hurling words like stones at one another, with the intent to inflict damage. She was well aware this was not what marriage was supposed to look like, but she didn't have a clue what to do about it.

That evening they intentionally put on happy faces before ringing the doorbell. Throughout supper they played their expected role as newlyweds, but later that night, as they'd gone to bed, tension still hung thick in the air.

With neither one willing to budge on their perspective, they'd eventually fallen asleep without resolving the matter, thus marking the beginning of a pattern that would prove fatal to their marriage: anger and arguing without resolution or reconciliation.

Over time, Jolene had felt the relentless winds of conflict further stripping away the hope and beauty from their marriage. Her heart ached now as she imagined the shattered dreams of all she'd once hoped for lying scattered at her feet, similar to the leaves beginning to pile up on the ground outside.

There had been many similar clashes over the years, often over her relationship with her parents or her desire to go back home for a visit. But they'd also done battle over trivial issues ranging from what she wore around the house or her hairstyle to his choice of music.

It had aggravated Jolene immensely when Tom wielded his role as spiritual head of the home by dictating how he wanted her to appear, yet neglected the role when it came to true leadership in spiritual disciplines like prayer, Bible Study, and modeling a Christ-like love for his bride. In her opinion, he held her and others to unfair, high standards to which he refused to hold himself.

It hadn't taken long to realize he was far from the best friend she'd always imagined her husband would be. Desperately, she'd done her best to change and mold him into the man she'd hoped for. Quick to speak her mind, she'd pointed out each trespass; voiced every disappointment. She felt he should know he wasn't meeting her expectations of what it meant to be a godly husband. Intending for her words to serve as constructive criticism motivating him to alter his behavior, she was frustrated when they appeared to fall on deaf ears.

More often than not, he'd responded by wordlessly heading out into the barn to tinker. Whether it was putting up chicken fence, re-wiring the barn, or anything else to keep him occupied, he'd often stay in the barn or yard all evening until she'd eventually make her way out to tell him she was heading to bed.

Depending on his mood, sometimes he followed her inside long enough to go through the motions of reading and praying with her before heading back out to the barn for a few hours. Other times he'd simply grunt, "G'night" without even glancing up from his work.

Somewhat out of a fear of vulnerability, but even more so because the focus of her prayers tended to be entreaties for God to change her husband's behavior, Jolene hadn't ever been overly eager or willing to pray out loud with Tom. Yet she strictly held to the belief he should read the Bible aloud with her each night before they knelt down at the bedside together, each offering an individual, silent prayer. It was what she'd witnessed her parents do and for her, there was simply a sense of security in the familiar ritual, regardless of the fact the tension between them as they kneeled was often so thick it could have been cut with a knife. She believed it was what Christian couples were expected to do so she made sure to remind him each night to fulfill his part of their "spiritual duty".

As the months had passed, Jolene repeatedly found herself in the role of an aggressive pursuer, although she was unaware her behavior had a label. Whenever there was tension, she wanted to confront and deal with it immediately so she could put it behind and move on.

It rankled that Tom, on the other hand, seemed to process things internally, behavior which she interpreted as the silent treatment. It baffled her how he thought anything could ever be resolved if it wasn't even discussed. In her opinion, his clamming up whenever there was tension seemed cowardly. But when she challenged him about it, he either blew off her concerns or, worse yet, responded with an angry outburst. When that happened the argument would quickly escalate into a heated exchange with so much damage inflicted that, no matter what the outcome, neither side ultimately came out a winner.

Jolene often wound up frustrated with herself for never seeming capable of choosing the right time for a confrontation. She wondered why they sometimes seemed to speak entirely different languages. But, not knowing how or what to change about her approach, she continued to pursue resolution on her timing. Looking back she had to admit her attempts at communication had hardly ever ended in harmony between the two of them.

In addition, beginning very early on, there had been intense battles over sexual intimacy...or more accurately, the lack thereof, in their marriage. They definitely had far different expectations in this area. Many nights Jolene would reject Tom's advances with one of several excuses such as: "Not tonight", "I don't feel like it", or "I'm too tired."

Sometimes the excuses were merely a cover up on her part for a much deeper need. As a woman, Jolene's heart hungered for an emotional connection with her husband. In order to be open to the physical act of sex, she first needed to know he cherished her. Instead, she often struggled with a profound lack of feeling loved, making it extremely difficult to give in to what she viewed to be selfish demands on his part.

Other times she would raise his hopes in the morning, indicating she might be open to intimacy that night. On those days, Tom went about his work with great anticipation, his thoughts repeatedly turned to Jolene, looking forward to going home to her that evening. Little did she realize how devastating it was to him when she would end up refusing his advances after all, perhaps because of something that had happened that day to shut her heart off towards him, or simply because she was no longer in the mood.

Worst of all, however, were the times she would grudgingly give in to his needs in a way that did very little to disguise the fact she was just enduring it for his sake and couldn't wait for him to finish the act and be done with it. To him this was the most demeaning of all.

Far from viewing intimacy as a beautiful gift from God, which she could give to her husband, Jolene grew to resent it as one more source of contention between the two of them. She seemed to have no clue what a deep need it was for Tom and how she was crushing and destroying him by physically withholding from him so often. Without a doubt, her naiveté in this area of marriage did untold damage to an already hurting relationship.

Eventually they had entered a season in their life when the storm clouds grew so dark their "house of cards" was beginning to collapse for the entire world to see.

With two toddler-aged girls and another child on the way, money had been growing tighter and tighter. Finally, Tom had decided to accept a job working four ten-hour shifts, from 4:00 p.m. to 2 a.m.

One fall day, not long after he'd begun working there, he and Jolene had been eating lunch together when Tom offhandedly mentioned a lady had moved from days to nights. Not once did it cross Jolene's mind that his unusual reference to this woman should be a red flag to her.

Because his shift ended long after bedtime, Jolene was rarely awake when he came home. However, one night shortly after Shayna had been born, Jolene noticed Tom's side of the bed was still empty when the sound of her newborn baby's cries woke her from an exhausted sleep.

Squinting at the clock on the nightstand, Jolene's heart raced when the blurry numbers came into focus.

Three twenty-nine a.m.!

Panic and fear began to rise up in her throat, and her heart raced as she debated who to call first; the police, his work, or his parents.

Thankfully, at that moment, she heard the familiar sound of his truck turning into the driveway.

Initially, all that registered was his apparent awkwardness at finding her sitting up, awake in bed. Then, in reply to her questioning look, he'd nonchalantly informed her he'd gone to Denny's with some of the guys after work. As her heart rate had returned to normal, she tried to think rationally and finally concluded it was a valid excuse.

That night hadn't been an isolated incident, however. Before long, it became routine for her to wake up and find herself alone in bed until three or four in the morning, sometimes even later. His excuses were always, "Out playing cards with the guys" or the now familiar, "At Denny's for breakfast, then playing basketball with some friends."

In her gut it didn't ring true.

But she still hadn't had a clue just how troubled their marriage really was.

Today, on their youngest daughter's birthday, Jolene was all too aware the changing of the seasons outside her window would continue to bring dramatic transformation to the landscape and eventually usher in the barrenness of winter. Likewise for her, that season in her life just a short time ago had transformed her heart, leaving it cold and bleak for a season.

———— ⟗ ————

Tom had broken the news in March.

It had been a sunny spring day and Jolene had made plans to spend the afternoon with her parents in the town of Morris, Illinois, a convenient meeting spot halfway between their homes. Always thankful for time with her family, she'd been in an upbeat mood that morning as she'd prepared for her road trip.

Until Tom gave her an ultimatum as she left.

It had been obvious for a long time he felt she was sharing too many details about their struggles with her parents. He'd accused her of painting him as the bad guy and didn't try to hide his opinion that his in-laws were too involved in their marriage, even hinting that the reason the two of them had never connected was because she wasn't willing to let go of the connection she had with her parents.

That day he took it a step further, making it abundantly clear he expected her to ask her parents to back off and leave them and their marriage alone.

Jolene had never stood up to her parents before. Besides that, she didn't think her parents were to blame for their problems. But, as she considered his ultimatum she saw it from a fresh perspective for the first time. Whenever Tom was sick or had a question regarding his food allergies, he tended to call his mom rather than turn to Jolene for advice or comfort. His argument that Jolene had never been sick enough to know the answers did nothing to appease her. Truth be told, she took it personally each time he sought his mom's input instead of hers. Processing all of this today, for the first time she had to admit she often did the same thing in return. She couldn't deny she had her dad on a pedestal and throughout marriage had often sought his advice before Tom's on a wide range of issues. If doing so made Tom feel at all like she did each time he ran home to his mom, she could appreciate a little more why he was making this demand of her today.

Based on her new understanding, and in order to save her obviously troubled marriage, she had made a very difficult decision to do as he'd asked. So that afternoon, during her time with her parents, she had been very frank and open with them, requesting that they give her and Tom the space he felt was necessary.

Although it had been a heart-wrenching conversation for her, as she'd driven home she had a sense of satisfaction that she'd done something Tom had asked of her and, by doing so, had shown him she was willing to place him above others.

Even those who meant so much to her.

She anxiously looked forward to sharing the news with him when he arrived home from work. But it was five a.m. the next morning before Tom walked into their bedroom.

Finding her awake, he cocked one eyebrow and questioned, "Well? Did you tell them?"

Expecting him to be pleased by her positive reply, she was completely confused when he responded with a miserable groan, as if his world had just fallen apart.

It wasn't until that afternoon she would come to understand Tom's groan had been a huge wave of guilt erupting from his chest as he realized his wife had finally listened to him and kept her part of the deal...just when he had utterly blown it and crossed a line he'd never intended to cross.

Without further conversation, he'd climbed into bed.

Pondering his strange response throughout the morning, Jolene had found herself more and more bewildered. So much so, the fact he hadn't gotten home until five o'clock in the morning hardly even registered in her mind.

But before Tom left for work again that afternoon, he'd asked Jolene to follow him to the garage, where he informed her they needed to talk.

A thousand thoughts flashed through her mind in an instant. It was as if all the red flags and suspicions she'd been subconsciously squelching for so many months were now fighting for center stage in her brain. Yet she still wasn't prepared for the words he uttered. Words that brought the bitterness of winter blowing into her heart with a vengeance.

He had been unfaithful.

Seeming strangely detached, Tom admitted he'd found himself in an emotional relationship with a woman from work for months; the same woman whom he had mentioned when she first started his shift. Playing with fire, they'd spent many hours together after work, enjoying one another's company and appreciating each other's attention. Although they'd placed themselves in compromising situations, he assured her they had kept from becoming physically intimate throughout the affair.

Until last night.

The very night Jolene had chosen to place her marriage above her relationship with her parents, he had allowed the final barrier to be broken down and crossed the last line standing, allowing the affair of his heart to become full-blown.

Even as his words were stabbing her heart, he twisted the knife even further with an implication that it was somehow her fault. In an accusatory tone, he'd informed Jolene it was because he didn't think she'd follow through on the ultimatum to tell her parents that he'd gone ahead and committed adultery that night.

As if her mind hadn't been reeling enough already, now she was also left trying to make sense of how on earth *she* was the one to blame for *his* hedonistic behavior. Deep down they both knew the real issue wasn't whether or not she had told her parents that night. He was using it as an excuse, but nevertheless the accusation found its mark and did its intended damage to her heart.

Waves of seething anger washed over her, immediately followed by torrents of gripping pain. Without realizing what she was doing, she began kicking the ground relentlessly, as if by doing so she could somehow stamp out the words he'd just uttered. Months later she would react in a similar manner when he broke the news about his plans to separate. For now, kicking up clouds of dust from the garage floor, she heard her own strangled voice repeatedly muttering, "I can't believe I never figured it out!"

Frustration at herself for not putting all the pieces together began to crash on top of the anger and pain like a tidal wave, overshadowing all other emotions.

She'd known their marriage was battered and bruised. She'd realized they were in trouble and even had her suspicions. But she'd never really imagined he would go so far as to cross this line. Never in a million years would *she* have considered having an affair. So she hadn't ever allowed herself to truly consider *he* might stoop to that level.

As Tom climbed into his truck and backed out of the driveway without any form of apology, the weight of his words began to sink in and she felt as if she was being crushed under a burden too heavy to bear.

Stumbling into the house, as if in a trance, she made her way to their bedroom and collapsed onto the bed. That's when the sobs came as she cried out to God, "Our lives will never be the same."

Words that had proven to be so true.

As news of Tom's infidelity inevitably spread throughout their family and community, Jolene had an odd sense of relief, realizing she could finally stop pretending everything was fine; at this point people were obviously aware life in the Young household was far from perfect! She had grown so weary of charades over the years that it was liberating to put the game on the shelf now that everyone knew their marriage was falling apart and her husband had been with another woman.

At the same time she experienced deep embarrassment over the public knowledge she hadn't been enough to keep her husband content. Worse yet was the inference by some that perhaps he had even been driven into the arms of the other woman by her own actions, indifference, or failures as his wife.

To be sure, she was far from innocent in the whole matter. She realized she hadn't loved or respected him like he'd wanted her to, nor had she babied him like he expected. But the night of his indiscretion she had kept her part of the deal they'd made, hadn't she? At least he couldn't hold that against her!

Unfortunately, she blew even that commitment a few days later. She'd been mid-sentence in a phone conversation when he'd shown up unexpectedly and caught her once again sharing details about him and their problems. His disappointment and anger at her betrayal of trust was immediately evident. In a raised voice he'd coldly informed her he would not be coming home that night. Then he'd turned on his heel and walked out the door without even a backwards glance. Moments later she'd heard him peeling out of the driveway.

Although there had been many times he had been gone into the wee hours of the morning, that night was the first he had ever shared his intentions prior to leaving. Jolene realized they had just reached a critical and devastating turning point. From the time his affair had been brought to light up until that afternoon he had been displaying signs of a repentant heart. But without a doubt her actions today had chased him away and into the arms of another! Sleeping alone that night, Jolene could blame no one but herself for her failure to keep a simple promise. Now all she could do was hope he would come home eventually and give her another chance to prove she could be trustworthy.

She was relieved when he had returned after a few nights away... but it had proven to be the beginning of a highly unpredictable roller coaster ride as Tom fluctuated between remorse and rebellion. Jolene never knew what to expect on any given day. Rarely did she know if he would even be sleeping in their bed or somewhere else entirely. But one positive that came from her failure to keep her promise was a strengthened resolve on her part to love him better than she ever had up to that point in their marriage.

Throughout all that time, from the humiliation of his affair becoming public, the subsequent church discipline and ensuing months of instability, one thing had sustained her: The constant, faithful love of Jesus. Even when she didn't recognize His loving arms carrying her through each day, He was there; her spiritual Bridegroom, the One who would never turn His heart away from her. He was completely trustworthy and would never let her down. If not for the safety of His Presence, she might not have survived those dark, bleak days of winter in her heart.

Now here she was, six months later, her marriage disintegrating even further with a pending separation only a few weeks away. She was dismayed at the prospect of having to pull the game of Charades back out of the closet and dust it off. But she saw no other way to deal with the day ahead.

With that thought in mind, Jolene put a smile on her face as her parents' car pulled in the driveway for the party. But as she checked her appearance in the mirror before going out to meet them, she was all too aware her smile didn't come anywhere close to reaching her eyes.

From an early point in their marriage, Tom and Jolene fell into a familiar trap. Attempting to disguise the dysfunction in their relationship, they put on a false front to those they were around. How often do we do the same thing, trying to cover our troubled

hearts with fake smiles? Unfortunately, even our churches are all too often filled with pretenders; Christians with pasted-on smiles, habitually blurting out, "I'm fine" when deep down they are anything but! It is a fact of life that this world brings trouble. Jesus warned us it would be so in John 16:33: "In the world you will have tribulation..." Yet He went on to encourage us, "...but be of good cheer, I have overcome the world." Perhaps our misunderstanding of the latter part of that verse contributes to covering up our pain; We assume if we are to be of good cheer, we can't let on to being battered and bruised by the inevitable waves of tribulation that crash upon us.

Believers definitely don't have an excuse to walk around downcast and without hope. In fact, Nehemiah 8:10b reminds us, "...Do not sorrow, for the joy of the Lord is your strength." Truly, very little brings more glory and honor to Christ than a follower who is able to cling to his or her joy in the midst of difficult circumstances. However, too often we give in to Satan's lies that we must always be strong, never allowing others to see our pain or weakness. In reality, hiding our hurts often leads to crippling isolation in the midst of our difficulties. Satan is the only winner as he craftily weighs us down with layer upon layer of guilt and accusation the longer we keep our sin and struggle in the darkness.

It seems what is lacking in far too many Christian circles today is true vulnerability stemming from genuine openness and honesty. Vulnerability can leave us feeling just like it sounds...exposed and bare. But if one brave soul is willing to bring their struggles into the light, amazing things inevitably happen. As soon as the facade of perfection is removed, others are freed to be real. Thus begins a beautiful manifestation of the Body of Christ, as members work together to encourage and carry one another across the valleys and back to the mountain tops.

Consider whether or not you may be hiding behind a mask of perfection today. If so, maybe it's time to remove it and watch what happens in your own life as well as those around you.

Chapter 5

———✦✕✦———

Shortly after Tom had admitted to his affair Jolene trusted it was over between him and his co-worker. But eventually she had become fairly certain he was again pursuing the other woman, although she didn't have any hard evidence with which to confront him.

Truth be told, at first she hadn't been sure she wanted to search for any, afraid of what she might find. However, before long, she could no longer resist the temptation to play detective and began checking his odometer in the morning. Knowing the mileage from home to his work and back, she felt her hands go clammy and cold the first time the numbers confirmed he'd driven much further than he should have.

Now, even as September rolled into October and their closing date approached, Jolene desperately tried to save what was left of their shattered marriage. She finally determined to do what it took to get Tom not only to come home, but also to stay. Even though he obviously wasn't putting any effort into rebuilding her trust, she tried to pour her heart out for him and the girls all the while being fully committed to leaving her family out of the picture. Making home a place he would desire to be, she went above and beyond anything she'd previously done.

If asked why she was giving so much of herself for his sake she would have answered, "Because it's what I'm supposed to." In her mind divorce just wasn't an option, so in order to save the relationship she was doing whatever she could to prevent that from happening.

Her efforts didn't go unnoticed by Tom. At one point he went so far as to tell her, "You are finally loving me the way I've always wanted to be loved!"

Unfortunately, in his mind it was a little too late. His heart was already made up.

Meanwhile, the stress began to take its toll on Jolene. She was physically and emotionally spent. With her stomach in knots most of the time and constantly battling intestinal issues, she had already lost fifteen pounds. Witnessing her weight loss and misery, Tom cavalierly remarked, "I guess it's *your* turn to suffer."

His comment was like a slap in the face, revealing just how much he viewed himself as the primary victim. Immediately bristling at the harsh remark, Jolene's first response had been, "How dare you say such a thing!" But she realized spouting off would send him out the door for the night so with great restraint she chose to hold her snide retort inside this time.

Even now, in the midst of this horrible mess, Jolene could see a silver lining to the dark clouds of despair. For in the darkness, even with her world crumbling under her feet, she felt herself on the verge of deeper spiritual growth. Since Tom had first mentioned separation, Jolene had started developing a relationship with her Lord like none she had ever known before; talking, communicating, and growing in the Word instead of just being caught up in tradition and other's expectations.

Prayer had always been an important spiritual discipline in her life, although it had often been performance driven; something she did out of duty or ritual more than a true conversation. But as she drifted through those days of uncertainty, prayer began to take on new meaning. When she felt at the end of herself she would send the girls out to the swing set in order to have some peace and quiet in which to think and pray. Digging deeper into God's Word, she found herself relying more on His presence than she ever had before.

She only regretted it had taken such drastic circumstances for her to finally begin this journey towards deeper spiritual maturity. The more her eyes were opened to Who God was, the more she realized just how shallow her spiritual understanding really had been and still continued to be.

Yet, even though relying on God the Father became more natural for her, it would still be awhile before her relationship would take on a deeper level of intimacy and friendship with His Son, Jesus. But it was definitely an improvement from what it had been for far too many years.

Unsure of Tom's real intent, and no longer able to trust him or his word, Jolene had sought out counsel and guidance for how to react to what was happening. There she had been told, "Just because Tom jumps out of an airplane without a parachute doesn't mean you have to, too." In a strange sense there had been comfort in those words; as if her fear and lack of trust in Tom were somehow validated.

She recalled a sermon she had heard years before, comparing a Christian's life to that of an air traffic controller. According to the minister, if an on-duty controller were to take his or her eyes off the computer monitors for only eight seconds, there was bound to be a crash. He then asked his listeners to consider how many times throughout the day they took their eyes off the Lord for eight second intervals or longer.

Now, almost six years later, Jolene could still remember the conviction she had felt that night as she wrote his analogy in her journal. At the time, she'd recognized the sobering truth: Far too often, she placed herself in peril by attempting to "fly solo", without having her eyes focused on her Creator.

There was a bittersweet consolation as she realized, in her present turmoil, turning to the Lord was becoming more instinctual for her.

Yet, in spite of it, life still felt like an unending nosedive. Would she ever be able to pull out of this free fall, she wondered?

Based on counsel from church leadership, and unbeknownst to Tom, she had found herself going through the surreal experience of contacting an attorney. At his suggestion, papers had been drawn up for a formal separation, in order to provide her with some level of financial protection in the days ahead.

How had life gotten so complicated that the one whom she'd vowed to love and cherish, through sickness and health, good times and bad, was considered so untrustworthy that she needed financial protection *from* and even *against* him? It seemed such a bitter irony.

Now, with a lump in her throat, and feeling every pounding heartbeat in her chest, Jolene rummaged through the kitchen drawer until she came across a pen that worked, throwing away a broken crayon and two dried out, capless markers in the process. Then, with shaking hands she went to locate Tom, suspecting he was going to be caught completely off guard by the papers she was about to give him.

Finding him in the living room, she asked if they could talk. He wordlessly rose and walked past her into the kitchen to grab a drink. Popping the can open, he pulled out a kitchen chair and dropped into it with a half-irritated expression on his face, waiting impatiently for what she had to say.

It was now or never.

Without a word Jolene tremblingly laid the formal papers on the table in front of him with the pen alongside. Wanting a little space between them, she backed away to the sink and began rinsing off dishes, all the while guardedly watching Tom skim the first page.

As she waited for a response, she recognized confusion flash across Tom's face first, followed immediately by shock and finally, unmistakable anger.

In spite of bracing herself for an outburst, she still hadn't been prepared for his reaction as he leapt to his feet and began spouting off at her. Wincing as his anger boiled over, and emotionally pummeled by the names spewing out of his mouth, she found herself speechless for once. For the first time ever, she feared his anger might even turn physical. So when he threw the pen across the room and stormed out the door without signing, her first emotion was relief. Slowly exhaling, she realized she'd been holding her breath.

In a daze, she heard his truck door slam, followed by the sound of peeling tires as he tore out of the driveway.

That's when the misgivings came rushing upon her. *What had she just done?*

No matter how much pain he had inflicted in four and a half years of marriage, no matter how bruised and beaten her heart, she still longed to make their marriage work. Hadn't she just assured him yesterday morning, "We can still work this out!"

No wonder he'd been shocked by her filing for legal separation just one day after that comment!

With doubts assailing her, Jolene turned once again to her new lifeline; prayer. Collapsing into the chair he'd just left, she laid her heart bare before her Lord like never before. Not only the thoughts she was able to articulate, but also the inward groaning of her spirit, to which she could put no words. Everything was placed at His feet in a desperate plea for grace, mercy, and wisdom.

Unaware how long she had been there, she suddenly realized it must be nearing suppertime. Yet she didn't rise from the chair until she felt the peaceful assurance of Christ's presence wash over her bleeding soul.

She truly believed He had been attentive to every word, both spoken and unspoken.

Although that knowledge didn't erase her problems, or make the path ahead of her a simple one, it somehow calmed her spirit. Suddenly, words she'd read that morning in Psalm 37:24 came to mind, "Though he fall, he shall not be utterly cast down; for the LORD upholds him with his hand."

Even now, she sensed the Lord, holding her hand, refusing to let go. She might stumble, and even fall, but He promised He would never desert her. No matter what lay ahead, she just needed to remain firmly in His holy grip and somehow, someway, she would make it through.

With that comforting thought, Jolene rose and began to rummage around in the fridge, looking for a simple meal to pull together. Thankfully, she found enough leftover mostaccioli to feed Shelby and Shania. With her own stomach in knots she certainly had no appetite, and Shayna could make do with some baby food. She was quite sure Tom wouldn't be back in time for supper. In fact, she wondered if he would even come home at all this evening or if he would eventually end up at his parents again, as he had off and on throughout the summer before.

While reheating last night's dinner and slicing up apples for her daughters, she felt a spiritual battle being waged in her mind. Despite the assurance she'd felt moments ago, fear was already trying to worm its way back in. Just because He promised to hold her hand and never let go didn't mean her future was all going to work out the way she hoped it would.

What if God actually had other plans besides putting the pieces of their broken family back together? Up until now she had always assumed that was His ultimate plan for them. What if it wasn't?

Jolene realized she had a choice. Would she give in to the hopelessness of the situation, or have faith to believe God had a purpose in the pain and it would all work together for good?

Pondering these questions, her eyes fell upon the daily calendar sitting on the windowsill above the sink. So many times throughout the past few weeks the verses on this flip calendar had spoken about grace, bringing deep comfort to her.

Today was no exception as the red-letter words of Christ jumped off the page, "My grace is sufficient for you: for my strength is made perfect in weakness." (2 Cor. 12:9)

No matter how desperate things appeared on the outside, and although she was still in turmoil, she knew she had to learn to peacefully rest in the sovereign control of her Savior. She had simple confidence He would take care of her, no matter what the future held for her and her daughters.

Many would say their marriage had suffered a fatal blow the night Tom committed adultery. Or even before that, throughout months of emotional unfaithfulness, not to mention the years of ongoing misunderstanding, unresolved conflict, lack of trust, and failure to love one another unconditionally. From a human standpoint, the death of their marriage seemed inevitable.

But deep in her heart, in spite of having handed Tom a paper requesting legal separation just a few hours before, she still held onto the belief that their marriage could be saved.

No matter how long it took.

Chapter 6

ires spinning on loose gravel, Tom slammed the truck into reverse and barreled down the country road towards town. Jamming his Guns N' Roses CD into the player, he cranked the volume up until the drumbeat vibrated through his ribcage.

Reaching into the glove box for a cigarette, he cursed when he realized he was out. It was almost time to head to work but he determined he would first stop for a pack at the gas station.

Up ahead he noticed an elderly man slowly moving towards the mailbox at the edge of the road. A few months before, Tom had found himself inwardly raging at this particular neighbor. All up and down his road lived staunch members of various conservative churches. Sober-minded to the core, this one especially seemed either unwilling or incapable of cracking a friendly smile or wave.

In his younger days Tom had held a deep respect for this type of individual, but now something about the extreme rigidness deeply annoyed him. So he had determined to elicit a neighborly wave each time they met, no matter how drastic he had to be in getting the man's attention. Thus, he'd begun a new pattern of relentless honking accompanied by frenzied waving. To his amazement, and even amusement, his scheme had worked! Several times recently he had received a wave, albeit reluctant, in return.

A bitter chuckle escaped Tom's lips as he anticipated the little routine about to take place. Still several hundred feet away, he laid one hand on the horn and began wildly waving with the other, a cheesy grin plastered on his face.

He watched cynically as the elderly man reached the mailbox, hesitated, and then almost imperceptibly raised his fingers in a sober salute.

Immediately, Tom released his hand from the horn and blew past, fully aware the reverberations of his music could not only be heard, but also felt, by the stunned man standing there watching him rocket past.

There had been a time, not so long ago, when he would have turned the volume down until he was out of earshot of this particular neighbor, or any others who would disapprove of his choice in music. In fact, for years, he had even kept a conservative a cappella CD in his glove box for the rare occasion when an individual with that mindset would ride with him. Although he preferred country music, he kept his preference to himself and was always prepared to place something more "acceptable" in the CD player, if he deemed it necessary.

Many times Jolene had pointed out the hypocrisy of his little facade, something that had only served to anger him further.

The differences in his and Jolene's musical preferences had been an unending source of contention throughout marriage. He could remember an incident in their first house that had proved just how big a pet peeve his choice of music was to Jolene. He had been listening to country music out in the garage and chatting with a friendly neighbor who had walked over when Jolene suddenly stormed out of the house, ripped the cord out of the wall and threw the whole stereo set into the garbage can. Without a word, she'd then spun on her heel and stomped back towards the house. Peering wide-eyed at Tom, the stunned neighbor had inquired somewhat hesitantly, "What just happened?" To which Tom had casually replied, "Oh, she doesn't like me listening to that kind of music." Then, going to the trashcan he had nonchalantly retrieved his stereo. Finding one speaker still worked, he'd plugged it back in and cranked up the volume in order to discourage any further questions from the flabbergasted neighbor.

Now as he thought back to that episode, he felt the same frustration he had back then. Why should she—or anyone else, for that matter—care so much what he listened to? Whose business was it, other than his own, what he chose to listen to in the privacy of his own home?

But then another question quickly made its way to the surface of his mind; if he didn't think there was anything wrong with it, why had he tried so hard to keep it a secret from so many people?

Truth be told, Tom had always been consumed with a fear of being confronted by someone who found anything about his lifestyle offensive. So he had attempted to keep his smoking, swearing, and music hidden, believing if no one knew, everything would be fine.

But how many times had Jolene pointed out just because his behavior went unseen by those who might take offence didn't make it excusable. She often reminded him how hypocritical it was to act one way while covering it up by pretending to be living another.

Next, she would throw out the kicker: He wasn't hiding anything from God, regardless!

Well, anymore he didn't give a rip! If his actions were disturbing to others, so be it. He was tired of living a life dictated by other people's expectations. His secrets were out, anyway, weren't they? In a community the size of theirs, news travelled fast and by now everyone and their dog knew his marriage was on shaky ground.

When he had admitted his adultery to Jolene several months before, he'd initially recognized the depth of his sin and had even been willing to confess it to church leadership. He still remembered the question posed by their church elder.

"Are you ready to go through the fire?"

Tom hadn't been sure what he meant at the time.

But it definitely hadn't been an easy road since then. There were days the heat had grown so intense, he'd felt he had no choice but to run from the scorching flames.

First there had been the disgrace of church discipline that spring. Because of the moral failure in his life, certain membership privileges had been removed. Worse yet, he had even been given the impression that he stood very little chance of ever being forgiven by God for what he had done, therefore there was little hope he'd ever be restored to full fellowship within the Body of Christ.

Daily he struggled with the question: had his adultery really caused him to forfeit his salvation and all hope of eternal life?

There were many who encouraged him otherwise, and tried to remind him of God's great compassion and unfailing mercy. All he needed to do was seek the Lord with a repentant heart in order to receive His full forgiveness.

Yet niggling doubts continued to surface now and then. At times the hopelessness that constantly dogged him drove him to despair and even deeper rebellion. If there was no hope for him spiritually then why even try to live a moral life anymore?

Other days he desperately longed for fellowship with God and his church family to be restored. With deep remorse for the choices he'd made, he would find himself in tears, wishing for days gone by when he'd had opportunities to serve within the Body of Christ. Looking ahead to the future, his heart yearned for the privilege of teaching his daughters' Sunday School classes. But by his actions he had relinquished that opportunity. Would he ever prove himself worthy of gaining any of it back?

Although he had been too humiliated to attend the church meeting when his sin had been made known, Jolene had done nothing to hide her opinion he should have been there that night, as she shared with him how much love had been poured out upon her. If he could have seen into her heart he would have realized she had even fed off the attention somewhat, interpreting many of the hugs and words of comfort as agreement with her that the lion's share of the blame fell upon Tom. In fact, the pity she received that night had seemed to reinforce her perspective of herself as victim.

Within a day or two of the meeting their mailbox began to fill up with cards of support, gifts of money, and words of encouragement for both of them, allowing him to experience firsthand the same love she had witnessed. Through that original outpouring from their church family, Tom's heart had softened and he'd mustered the strength to attend the following Sunday, bravely facing those whom he had let down.

Yet, in spite of the initial regret and sorrow over what he had done, within a matter of days his heart had grown colder and he'd found himself back in the arms of the woman from work.

He also found another mistress who helped, temporarily, to numb the pain in his heart: Alcohol.

Many nights he found himself purchasing a case of beer then spending his evening sitting on the couch, nursing his wounds with can after can, oblivious to the fact his wife was trying in her own way to heal the wounds he'd inflicted in her life.

To be honest, he no longer felt responsible or accountable to Jolene. It was almost as if his conscience had been seared to the point he no longer felt any guilt. Some nights he stayed out until five a.m., nonchalantly ignoring Jolene's questioning looks upon his arrival home. Other times, rather than facing up to the disappointment and accusation in her eyes, he'd simply crash at his parents for a few hours before returning to work. Sometimes he'd even bunk at their house for a few days at a time.

Rarely did he feel the need to fill Jolene in on his plans. He was living a life of self-indulgence without considering the ramifications of his actions upon anyone else.

In recent years, Tom's spending had grown out of control. Within a short period of time he had purchased a fancy CD player, motorcycle, truck, brand new TV, cable service, a huge library of music, stacks of movies, and much more, including a pack of cigarettes on a regular basis. Altogether, he had racked up thousands of dollars of credit card debt. Shortly after Shania had been born he had felt it was time to upgrade the family car to a minivan, even though they really couldn't afford the additional payment along with their mortgage payment and other debts. Once he began drowning his guilt in alcohol, he put further strain on their budget.

In fact, their finances had reached a crisis point around the time of his excommunication from church. When one of the ministers had asked Jolene if there was any tangible way to help out she had sheepishly admitted their financial troubles. Subsequently, for three months in a row, their church family had blessed them with money to assist in making house and van payments. The monetary gifts had brought about mixed emotions in Tom, not the least of which was shame. Although he wasn't willing to admit his foolish spending habits were mainly to blame for the condition they were in, he was ashamed that he was unable to adequately provide for his own family. Accepting the money also made him feel somehow indebted to the congregation; a fact that he resented at a time when he desired to distance himself from them.

Now, just moments after walking out on Jolene's request for his signature on the separation papers, Tom peeled into a gas station and hopped out of the truck, leaving his keys in the ignition. His thoughts still ran rampant, hashing over the past few months of life. As he plunked money down on the counter to pay for a package of cigarettes his mind returned to the paper Jolene had set before him moments before.

What irked him the most was her request for both alimony and child support. If he had his way, he would never give in to such a selfish request from her. Yes, the girls were partly his responsibility and he realized he needed to help cover expenses for them. But Jolene? Why should he have to pay *her*? In his current state of mind it made absolutely no sense to give anything more than absolutely necessary to Jolene.

There was a lot he was unsure about these days. But one thing he knew for certain as he headed to work.

It was time to go talk to an attorney. Because there was absolutely no way he was going to sign anything as ridiculous as the document Jolene had laid in front of him today!

Chapter 7

Although Jolene had procrastinated and put off the inevitable as long as possible, earlier in the week she had finally begun the difficult process of packing up, along with the help of some friends. Today they would finish the ordeal of dividing their belongings and emptying their house of its final contents.

Just a week previously, her parents had driven down early on Sunday morning, bringing an empty trailer in which they planned to take an initial load of larger items back to Elgin. Instead of going on the pulpit as a visiting minister that day, her dad had chosen to sit in the audience alongside Tom and his dad. Jolene had glanced over mid-service to see her husband, father, and father-in-law all sharing one bench. Time seemed to freeze as she captured a picture of the three of them in her mind; a picture she would remember for years. In just a few hours she and Tom would be splitting up their earthly belongings, marking the true beginning of their separation. But for this moment she could almost fool herself into believing everything was normal.

After church that day her mom had graciously made supper and watched the girls while Tom and Jolene sorted furniture, deciding which pieces he would keep and which should be loaded onto the trailer for her and the girls. Then, with the help of her dad, they went about the business of loading the heavy pieces.

Throughout the afternoon Jolene had been struck by how civil she and Tom were managing to be towards one another in the midst of such a tense situation, often deferring to the other one in their decision making. If they were able to treat each other with so much respect today, of all days, wasn't there hope they could still work their marriage out?

Finally, as the seven of them had gathered around the dinner table for supper, her dad had spoken for everyone when he'd pondered out loud, "Are you two really sure you want to go through with this? You seem to be getting along very well!"

After a few seconds, Tom broke the awkward silence with nothing more than a wry chuckle. Then everyone resumed eating as if the question hadn't been asked and there was nothing bizarre about peacefully enjoying a meal together in the midst of dividing all they had into two separate households.

Having survived round one, it was now time for round two. Over the past few months Jolene had grown rather accustomed to awkward moments, but this day promised to hold even more than she felt emotionally equipped to handle. Her whole family was on their way to help pack up the final trailer of belongings Jolene would be taking with her while the rest would be going on a second trailer for Tom. She imagined the air would be thick with tension as her family worked alongside Tom and some of his family emptying the house of all they had accumulated in five and a half years of marriage.

But her fears had been unfounded for once.

By lunchtime, as Jolene was making a mental checklist of all that still needed to be done, she realized how peaceful the morning had actually gone. From the moment her parents and siblings arrived, she'd noticed a generous spirit flowing between everyone. Although she knew her family members were battling their emotions and had to be struggling with the task at hand as well as their feelings towards Tom, they had been very cordial when he had shown up. In fact, they were treating him with the utmost kindness and courtesy as everyone pitched in together.

Jolene's respect and appreciation for her father had grown by leaps and bounds the prior week and continued to do so today as she observed him working alongside his son-in-law, cleaning out the barn and loading tools and boxes from the garage onto Tom's trailer. She could only imagine how much his father-heart wanted to lash out protectively with, "How could you do this to my daughter and granddaughters?" She marveled as she watched him graciously carry another box without a word of complaint, carefully sliding it into the trailer bed of the man who had trampled his daughter's heart. Little did she know at one point that day her dad had pulled Tom aside and quietly reminded him, "You know it doesn't have to be this way!" When Tom hadn't responded he had wisely dropped the issue.

As the day progressed, Jolene struggled with a jumble of emotions. All the hurt, anger and disillusionment from the past few years begged to surface and demand some justice for all Tom had put her through. But she also sensed that little seedling of hope, though buried deeply, still trying to survive.

Throughout the day, she found herself watching Tom for any signs of remorse, sadness, or regret. However there was none that she could detect. She was struck by the matter-of-fact manner in which he relinquished even the sentimental memorabilia, encouraging her to place it all in "her" stash. She had the sense he wanted absolutely no reminders of their life together.

Carefully packing their wedding album and family photos into a box together before sealing it shut with tape, Jolene battled an overwhelming sadness.

This was for real. Life, as she knew it, was over. Those frightening thoughts that had pressed down on her the night he'd told her of his affair now washed over her again. "Life will never be the same."

It hadn't been and never would again.

By late afternoon, the house was just an empty shell, waiting for its next occupants. While the women had cleaned and vacuumed inside, Tom, his grandpa and father-in-law had worked on the outbuildings and now everything was fresh and sterile. Void of anything personal, or of anything at all for that matter, the house felt cold and lonely.

Jolene shivered as she walked outside to thank everyone for their help. Her parents were ready to leave with the trailer containing her half of their goods. They planned to haul all Jolene's belongings to their house, which she and the girls would be calling "home" for the time being. She was overwhelmed with awe and gratitude for her family's assistance and unfailing support, not just today but throughout this whole ordeal.

After watching everyone pull out, Jolene stepped back into the empty kitchen while the girls waited for her in the van. With no chairs or table left, she joined Tom at the counter, where they stood to write checks for all their outstanding bills. Then it was time to leave their house for the final time.

Tom walked through the door nonchalantly, without any apparent struggle or so much as a glance around him. But as Jolene stepped outside of their home and began to pull the door shut one last time, she found herself hesitating. No matter what the future held, she was fully aware once she shut this door a chapter in her life would be firmly closed.

Jolene felt a battle raging deep inside, as if she could ward off the inevitable by not turning the page. She could simply refuse to attend the closing or sign the papers on Monday. Tom was obviously making a terrible mistake. Surely he'd come to his senses and realize that one of these days, wouldn't he? Shouldn't she do whatever she could to prevent him from causing further shipwreck in his own life, as well as hers? What about the girls? Was there something she could do to prevent any further scars in their tender hearts? What was going to happen to all of them during this time of separation? How long would it take before they would be back together as a family? What would it take?

Even as the questions raced through her mind, Jolene's hand pulled the door shut and gave it an extra little jiggle, purely out of habit. Locked. Never to be opened again by either of them.

Moving away from the house and heading to their vehicles without a word, Jolene recognized the irony of the moment. It seemed oddly fitting, in a symbolic way, that just as their family was now divided in two, they were driving away separately from the house they'd purchased as a couple.

Tom's grandparents generously opened their home to Jolene and the girls that evening. She was grateful for their kindness and relieved that the girls had somewhere they felt comfortable to spend the first night away from home. Everyone was exhausted after an emotionally and physically draining day, making for a much smoother bedtime routine than she'd anticipated.

The next morning Jolene and the girls attended church in Forrest one last time then headed to a gathering with an out-of-town potluck group she and Tom had been part of for most of their marriage.

After supper and dessert, Tom showed up to see the girls one final time before they left. Jolene had decided to stay in Forrest for a few more days, and Shelby would be staying with her, but Shania and Shayna were going to catch a ride back to Elgin with Jolene's cousin and her family that evening.

Not able to bear watching Tom say his goodbye, she busied herself with the job of gathering her two younger daughters' belongings together. All too soon it was her turn to hug and kiss them before sending them on their way with promises to be together again very soon. As the car pulled away, they excitedly waved from the backseat. Jolene was amazed by their resilience. To their innocent minds, getting to go live with Grandpa and Grandma for awhile was equivalent to a grand adventure!

As soon as Tom finished his goodbye with Shelby, Jolene loaded her up and they headed to a friends' house, where they planned to spend the next few days. With the closing to attend the next day, she was grateful Shelby would be taken care of.

Glancing in the rearview mirror at her eldest child, she wondered how much Shelby was struggling. Although generally cheerful she was somewhat reserved by nature, so it wasn't unusual for her to keep her thoughts to herself. But lately she'd seemed even quieter, as if she were processing everything internally. Perhaps the two of them having some time together before they met up with the rest of the family would be beneficial. Jolene determined to focus on Shelby the next few days, trying to get a feel for how her sweet four year old daughter was truly adjusting to all the dysfunction.

For most people, purchasing or selling a house is a joyous occasion; cause for great celebration. But there was a somber tone in the room as they met their banker, realtor and the purchasers the next afternoon. The conversation was kept business-like while they signed an endless number of papers then waited as their mortgage was paid off and joint checking account closed out. Eventually, they were each handed an envelope with the remaining cash divided between them.

The time had come to go their separate ways.

Nowhere is there a manual that teaches one spouse how to turn and walk away from the other without so much as a single backward glance. The most reliable of all marriage manuals, The Holy Bible, instructs how to walk *together* through life, moving *towards* one another, not away from. So they were in unchartered water that afternoon as they stood outside the bank, with their separate envelopes of cash.

What would be appropriate for such an occasion? Business partners and even mere acquaintances share a handshake as farewell. Tom and Jolene had shared a home, a family, even a bed with one another...but now, in a surreal moment, they walked away without a single touch or even so much as a lingering glance into one another's eyes.

With a casual, "Well, see ya!" Tom simply turned, climbed into his truck, drove off and was gone.

Could it really be as simple as that?

Following five and a half years of marriage, could they really just walk away from one another like absolute strangers, acting as if there was nothing between them; had never been, and maybe never would be again?

There are times in life when the emotion of the moment is too deep to fathom and the body must go into auto pilot in order to survive. For Jolene, this was one of those times. It was impossible to know what to do or think. Should she stand here awhile longer, waiting for a miracle; a Hollywood ending in which he would get to the corner, turn around, jump down from the truck and run towards her in slow motion, taking her in his arms and assuring her he had been wrong and that they could work it all out?

Or should she be thankful to have some time away from him and all the pain he had inflicted upon her?

Finally, feeling foolish about the possibility of being caught staring in the direction he had just driven, she climbed into her van and laid the envelope on the seat beside her. Then, once again, she found herself turning to the one and only thing she could; prayer.

As she drove to her friend's home, she prayed for wisdom to know how to explain everything to Shelby today, as well as Shania and Shayna in the days ahead when the questions were sure to come. She prayed for guidance to know how to move on with her life and strength to carry on. She prayed for provision for their earthly needs and protection for all of them from whatever lay ahead.

And last of all, she prayed for a miracle. Not just a Hollywood miracle; instead she prayed for a miracle of Heavenly proportions.

Chapter 8

After spending a week in the Forrest area, Jolene and Shelby traveled to Elgin. Pulling into the driveway of her childhood home had felt like a bizarre dream. How could it be she was coming back, not for a visit, but as a desperate, single mom in need of a place to live?

Not wanting to upset Shelby, she'd tried to keep her reaction hidden but had felt her stomach tighten in knots as she parked the van, unloaded baggage and carried it inside.. Assailed by feelings of failure, she could almost imagine a neon "Single Mom" sign with a flashing arrow pointing directly at her, drawing the attention of anyone who happened to glance her way.

After several weeks in her parent's home, Jolene and the girls were adjusting to a new routine. Yet mornings were still painfully difficult. Jolene had never been a morning person. In fact, she had written in her journal during her college days how much she hoped whomever she married would understand and be patient with her distaste for morning. Yet, nothing compared to the miserable feeling of waking up morning after morning in her former bed at her childhood home, without her husband. After her two brothers had become engaged, but before her own engagement, there had been days when the loneliness of single-hood had pressed down hard upon her. But the present loneliness she felt, with her husband hours away in another bed, and no idea if he was alone or not, sometimes seemed as if it would crush her.

Almost immediately, Jolene's dad hired her as a plumber for his business. It was work she enjoyed and, better yet, working for the family business provided a "safe" environment where she was surrounded by the compassion of those who loved her. Being back in her hometown, she never lacked the supportive presence of friends or family.

Still, there were plenty of awkward moments when she would run into an acquaintance who had not yet heard the news of her and Tom's situation. Because the legal separation had not been finalized, she wasn't even sure how to describe her marriage status when asked. Deep in her heart she still held out hope for reconciliation, so there were times she didn't bother to explain at all, just allowed the other party to assume she was visiting the Elgin area without Tom.

Since she'd left Elgin, life had changed considerably for not only her, but also everyone else. Her family had grown and her brothers now had families of their own. Most of her single friends from the past were married, with children. As a mom of three young girls, participating in the church's youth group activities was undeniably awkward. On the other hand, although young couples and families often tried to include her in their activities, without a husband her presence created an odd number and she grew to despise the distinct feeling of being a fifth wheel.

Many nights she felt her heart crying out to God, "Just where do I belong?" In those lonely moments she was so grateful for the one relationship that hadn't changed. She was, and always would be, the daughter of a King. Married or single, mom or not, her status didn't make any difference when it came to her relationship with her Heavenly Father. It was that constant comfort which carried her through the painful transitions in those first few weeks.

On November 26th, Jolene found herself facing Tom once again; this time in court.

Making the drive to Pontiac for their first appearance, her hands tightly gripped the steering wheel as she fought off conflicting emotions at a dizzying rate.

Frustration towards herself battled for a place amongst all the anger towards Tom. Had she not filed for a legal separation, there wouldn't even be a need for this trip to court. But ultimately, she had to admit this whole mess was Tom's fault anyway. If he hadn't forced her hand, she would never have considered taking such a drastic step. She was just doing it to protect herself and the girls.

In spite of her anger and doubts, the nearer she came to her destination, the more she realized deep down in her heart what she desperately longed to do was walk into that courtroom, look Tom in the eye and beg him to forget all the drama. She wanted to convince him they could still make it work if only they'd go home, together, and start all over.

Turning into the courthouse lot she parked and spent a few quiet moments calling out to God for strength to survive whatever lay ahead. Then, with a reluctant heart she stepped out of the van and went inside to meet her attorney.

Once their case was called, everything became a blur. She heard but wasn't sure she understood when Tom's attorney filed a motion for temporary relief of separation, wrapped in a lot of legalese.

Jolene's brain was trying to process why Tom would be fighting the separation. Did this mean he was having second thoughts and hoping to reconcile? Was he finally coming to his senses?

Her heart pounded so loudly she wondered if the judge could hear the thumping. Glancing at Tom, she tried to read the expression on his face but it held no clues. Other than a distinct sense he was intentionally avoiding her eyes.

Within another minute the hearing was over and Jolene left the courtroom more confused than ever. She received no answers from Tom or his attorney as they briskly walked away without a word of acknowledgement.

But it hadn't taken long for Tom's intent to become clear. Within a few days she had received by mail a counter petition for dissolution of marriage. Understanding dawned as Jolene processed the words on yet another legal document.

She finally realized what Tom was doing. Not willing to lose the upper hand in their unfolding drama, he had obviously decided to deliver a final blow by forging ahead and filing for divorce, rather than give her the satisfaction of the legal separation she had requested. It seemed obvious he wanted to remain in control of the situation.

Thunderstorms generally begin brewing from one small gust of wind, which grows in intensity and power. Similarly, Jolene felt a sense of rage and injustice beginning to form and grow within her being. The words on the page became a swirling blur as one question bubbled to the surface of her mind:

How dare he do this?

After all, hadn't it been Tom who had failed in his role as spiritual head from the beginning of their marriage? It seemed he had always been more concerned about what others might think than about growing to understand his wife's heart. Self-righteous anger rose up within Jolene. How many sacrifices had *she* made, how many times had she offered a second and even third chance? *He* was the one who had the affair, for goodness sake! Hadn't she stuck by his side through it all, working to love him better afterward than she had before? And this was what she received in return!

The more Jolene considered all the struggles they'd gone through the past few years the more indignant she became.

When Tom had struggled with a debilitating depression that finally ended in hospitalization, hadn't *she* spent time visiting him, demonstrating she cared and wanted to help? When he'd admitted the affair, instead of giving up on him, hadn't *she* chosen to stick it out and try to forgive? Throughout all those late nights last summer when he never came home, *she* was always there waiting when he finally did decide to return, usually with little or no explanation for where he'd been.

If either of them had the "right" to divorce the other, wasn't *she* the one who did? Yet through it all, not once had she allowed herself to even consider divorce as an option. So how could he do this now, especially when she was still offering him every opportunity to work things out and get back together?

For the next few weeks, Jolene found every waking moment haunted by these questions until the rage had grown and was beginning to consume her. Icy cold fingers of bitterness clamped tighter around her heart each day. Her focus turned further inward as she perceived herself more and more in the role of victim. As December marched on, she found herself laying more and more blame at Tom's feet, pointing fingers at him in her mind whenever memories would surface.

Rarely did she allow herself to consider the possibility of any blame on her part. It was so much simpler to be angry with Tom for all the pain he'd inflicted than to let the light of Truth shine into her own heart and force her to take responsibility for her personal actions.

Even her Bible reading seemed to justify her feelings towards him as she read God's commands to live holy and righteous lives. Hadn't Tom fallen short in so many ways? Many days her quiet time in the Word of God was spent as if looking through a window at all of Tom's failures, rather than allowing the Word to be a mirror through which she recognized and confessed her own shortcomings.

So even as her dependence on God deepened and her relationship with Him took on new meaning, she sensed a barrier growing between herself and her Lord, but was unable or unwilling to put her finger on the reason for the increasing distance.

She was spending so much more time in His presence, relying on the promises of the Bible and communion with Him in prayer as a lifeline. Yet even as she cultivated the tender seedlings of hope and trust, watering them with the Word regularly, she sometimes had the impression they were being choked out by something bigger. It would be several years before the root of bitterness springing forth in her soul would be weeded out entirely and cast aside. Until that time it grew many tendrils that at times threatened to entirely strangle the fruit of the Spirit.

Following a noticeably subdued Christmas celebration, Jolene found herself making another trip to Pontiac for the first divorce court hearing. As she drove, frustration once again engulfed her. In spite of all the bitterness in her heart, she knew without a doubt divorce just wasn't the answer.

Upon arriving at the courthouse, she was dismayed to find the four of them; Tom, Jolene and their two attorneys, forced to remain in the hallway until they were called into the courtroom. While waiting, she wrestled internally for several minutes before finally working up the courage to approach Tom and ask for a private word with him. Feeling she had to make one last attempt to reach him, she humbled herself enough to ask yet again, "Are you *sure* you want to go through with this?"

The irony of the moment wasn't lost on her, and a part of her despised how desperate it made her appear, especially when his curt reply of, "Yes, I'm sure!" was quickly followed by the click of his dress shoes on the wooden floor as he abruptly returned to his spot beside his attorney.

But she also felt better for having tried.

That day in court proved to be simply a formality and she left with little more than another court date two months down the road and a sick stomach. Seeing Tom's nonchalance had stirred her anger, as well as brought fresh waves of pain and humiliation. But through it all she took comfort in knowing *she'd* tried again today to make him stop the foolishness.

At least no one would ever be able to blame *her* for this divorce!

Chapter 9

*J*t has been said that all sin comes with a price but Satan is crafty enough to keep his hand on the price tag until after we fall. Such was the case with Tom. Initially, the headiness of freedom blinded his eyes to the exorbitant costs to him and his family. All he knew was that after years of feeling stifled, he finally felt unshackled!

He was free from responsibility, conflict and meddling; liberated from discouragement, conviction and finger pointing. He was no longer accountable to a wife, family, in-laws, or even a church. He knew he was walking in defiance to God but felt absolutely no responsibility or accountability to Him, either.

He could do *what* he wanted, *when* he wanted, *how* he wanted...and answer to no one!

As he walked away from it all, he sensed stress and worry flow off his back. More than once he found himself wondering why he hadn't done this long before! This new, carefree lifestyle was invigorating. At last released from the pressure of trying to please others, he grew to care less and less what anyone thought of him. In fact, he sometimes found himself purposefully trying to stun others with his actions, just for the shock value.

Gaining the upper hand in the legal process was important to Tom so, upon meeting with his attorney, he had decided to go all the way and file for divorce in response to Jolene's request for separation.

He justified his actions through severely twisted reasoning: Since they had never shared a true connection with one another or experienced what he believed to be a "real" union, he argued that their marriage theoretically hadn't even existed. Because of this, in his mind the step from legal separation to divorce had seemed rather insignificant and impacted him very little, emotionally.

Surprisingly, he didn't feel the slightest twinge of guilt. But if he had, he was sure he could have easily drowned it with alcohol.

The downward spiral had begun as a slow descent, with binging only on the weekends. But the longer he and Jolene were separated, the more frequently he began heading to the bars, until it became an every night occurrence.

Except for when the girls were at his house.

From the beginning he and Jolene had agreed to share time with the girls, so every other weekend he would meet her partway and get Shelby, Shania, and Shayna for a couple days.

Putting on the mantle of responsibility for a weekend was tolerable and he truly enjoyed spending time with his three young girls who were four, three and one at the time.

The possibility his actions could be inflicting damage on his precious daughters rarely, if ever, even crossed his mind. In his opinion, being part of a broken or blended family was just an accepted and normal family dynamic. He was convinced his girls would turn out fine in spite of being raised by separated or divorced parents.

The first weekend they had swapped the girls it had warmed his heart immensely to witness how excited his daughters were about the privilege of spending a weekend at their dad's new place. He had tried to make it a special time, purchasing a whole cupboard full of snacks just for them and stocking up ahead of time on new "girly" things he thought they would enjoy, including purses, a box full of costume jewelry, as well as a stash of dress-up hats.

The weekend had gone so well, in fact, Tom couldn't help wondering if the girls were perhaps better off with this new arrangement than they had been living in a house with two parents who argued all the time.

He found it difficult not to gloat a little when it came time to meet Jolene again on Sunday night. Although the girls had all bounced right out of their mom's vehicle and into his on Friday night, now Shelby was in tears, clinging to him and refusing to let go. His oldest daughter obviously wanted to stay with him instead of go back home with her mom, much to Jolene's dismay and his own barely concealed amusement.

As months passed, and the swapping of custody became more of a routine, there were times Tom sensed Jolene attempting to send him on a guilt trip regarding the effect his decisions were having on the girls. Her finger-pointing, whether perceived or actual, never failed to raise his temper to a boiling point. Often those moments of rage would drive him to the bottle, although he was careful to stick to his self-imposed limit of one beer whenever his daughters were around.

Once he had them safely deposited back to their mom, he would allow himself to completely douse his anger with booze. In order to avoid a confrontation, he sometimes would ask his parents to meet Jolene so he didn't have to. Although he was no longer accountable to her, something about seeing his estranged wife on a Friday afternoon tended to dampen his spirits for the rest of the weekend. Instead of acknowledging the possibility it could be his conscience stinging him, Tom attributed his negative feelings to all the deep-seated baggage associated with Jolene from the never-ending conflict that had consistently permeated their marriage.

Of course Jolene made very little effort to disguise her opinion that sending his parents was a cop out. They were *his* kids and she clearly felt *he* should be the one shuttling them back and forth. But sensing Jolene's critical attitude only reinforced Tom's desire to avoid her, giving him further reason to send his parents in his place.

February 11ᵗʰ, 2003 Tom woke with a sense of determination. Carefully choosing his attire with the intent to impress, he pulled out one of his suits from the back of the closet and grabbed a tie to match. Pressing a white shirt, he realized it had been almost a year since he'd been dressed this way. As a matter of fact, the last time he'd worn a suit had been his final appearance at church with Jolene. Back then, she'd kept his shirts neatly ironed for him. Pressing the spray button in an attempt to steam out a stubborn wrinkle, he wished he'd asked his mom to do this job. Or taken the shirt to the cleaners.

Once he was dressed, he gathered his growing file of paperwork regarding the legal separation and now-pending divorce. Then, almost as an afterthought, he rummaged around in the closet until he found his briefcase. Dusting it off, he slid the folder inside. Determined the judge wouldn't consider him a good-for-nothing, negligent husband and father, he was pleased with what he saw when he glanced at himself in the mirror. Even he was impressed with the air of professionalism he portrayed.

In stark contrast to Tom's smug optimism heading into court that day, Jolene was waging an emotional battle with herself as she made the two-hour drive from Elgin to Pontiac. She had no doubt Tom and his attorney would rake her over the coals, blaming her as much as possible for the failure of their marriage. Yet she was unsure how to mentally prepare for the questions and accusations she was sure to face in the courtroom.

The more she thought of what Tom might say, nagging guilt began working its way into her mind, pointing accusatory fingers at her. Over the years there had been many occasions when she'd sensed Tom blaming her for not being the wife he'd hoped she would be. Now her mind began to wander down a path of imagining how differently things might have turned out if only she had been "enough" for him. A voice whispering in her ear repeatedly reminded her if she had been more adequate in every way he wouldn't have needed to go elsewhere for companionship.

As the gnawing guilt began to press down heavily upon her, out of the blue a phrase she'd been told once came to mind. "Guilt is not a *feeling*, it is a *position*." The fact was, in spite of any accusations or charges Tom might bring against her, in reality he was not the one with the ability to declare whether or not she was guilty. Nor was the earthly judge before whom she would stand today. Ultimately, the Bible was the Law and God was the final Judge. Her responsibility was to read and apply the Word, allowing it to shine light on any sin in her own life that needed to be dealt with.

Healing truth began to wash over her heart and mind as she fought off Satan's attacks with the comfort of God's promises. According to His Word, the cleansing blood of Jesus provided forgiveness for all the sins she had already laid at the foot of the cross. She could no longer be held in a position of guilt for what God had deliberately chosen to forget forever. Nor could she be responsible for vague feelings of regret and insufficiency. Considering these truths lifted her spirits immensely.

Contemplating forgiveness, Jolene had a vague sense of conviction and realized perhaps she needed to do a sincere soul searching to determine if she was harboring any sinful attitudes towards Tom in her heart. But not having the emotional strength to fully devote to it right then, she drove the rest of the way focusing instead on some of her favorite Bible verses, especially Isaiah 26:3: "You will keep him in perfect peace, whose mind is stayed on You, because he trusts in You." For today her greatest challenge would be to keep her mind focused on Christ, trusting the outcome to Him.

When she pulled into the parking lot she was considerably calmer than she had been when she began her journey that morning. Gathering her purse and stack of papers, she noticed Tom's empty truck a couple rows over. He was obviously already inside. Drawing in a deep breath, she locked the van and walked towards the building. As she did, she reminded herself, if God had brought her to this moment He would surely see her through.

Tom had arrived a few minutes early that morning. Shaking hands with his attorney in the hallway, he purposely kept his eyes from searching for Jolene amongst the others milling around, waiting a turn in the courtroom. No need to get that unsettled feeling he so often did when he saw her.

Once their case was called, he gave a curt nod in her direction as they entered the courtroom and each took their places beside their respective attorneys at the front tables. He couldn't help but feel more than a little superior as he considered his briefcase compared to her simple stack of a file, notebook and pen.

Tom was called to the stand first, where his lawyer peppered him with questions. Because he had been the one to file for divorce, the burden of proof lay upon him. Ignoring the shame and humiliation of airing so much dirty laundry in front of the judge, attorneys, and all the others in the room, he tried his best to portray the "cruelty" he had endured and the frustrations he'd dealt with for five years of marriage.

He described in detail the way Jolene had pestered and nagged him about his smoking, music, purchases; even his relationship with his parents. He also shared the lack of intimacy in their marriage; both in frequency and interest level on Jolene's part. It seemed no subject was too private to be touched upon, in spite of all the strangers sitting behind him.

Then it was Jolene's turn to answer his attorney's questions and defend her behavior. Over the course of the next half hour or so, they took turns hashing out their differing interpretations of church traditions and marital issues. Jolene used church and religion as her defense, reminding the judge that she hadn't placed any unusual demands upon Tom. All that she had expected of him was consistent with his upbringing and in line with what he had embraced by choosing to become a part of their denomination.

After hearing both sides, it didn't take long for the judge to determine the outcome.

With a bang of his gavel, he dismissed their case.

Based on the arguments he had heard from each of them, he had denied Tom the right to divorce Jolene on the chosen grounds of "mental cruelty and unusual punishment", making it quite clear that Tom's complaints had failed to convince him Jolene's behavior had been sufficiently cruel *or* unusual.

Walking out of the courtroom more than a little deflated, Tom waited in the hallway while his attorney gathered files and caught up with him. As they strode through the door and out into the brisk winter air, he overheard Jolene's attorney off-handedly inform her they were the first couple in the history of Livingston County to have a divorce denied.

Not exactly the type of notoriety Tom was looking for!

As he climbed into his truck, he caught a final glimpse of Jolene walking towards her van. He was thankful he was too far away to make out her expression, not wanting to chance the possibility of spotting even the slightest hint of victory in her eyes.

Driving off, he realized the fight was far from over. He wasn't about to give up just because of some judge's order! As a matter of fact, being denied the right to divorce was like a fresh fire under Tom, driving the desire even deeper within him. So, shortly after the disappointing outcome in court and based on his attorney's recommendation, Tom had decided to switch legal grounds from mental cruelty to irreconcilable differences. This change would require much less proof on his part.

However, it also came with a mandatory two-year waiting period.

He was willing to wait that long, fully convinced divorce was the next step on his path to complete freedom.

In the meantime, he received a notice that Jolene was petitioning him for $1000 of monthly alimony. The news had about caused him to blow a gasket. In fact, the boldness of it had enraged him so much he'd immediately called her up to speak his mind.

Once he heard her voice on the phone he lost his temper and called her a choice name, something that had been a rarity, even in spite of the constant bickering between them. Without waiting for a response from her, he hung up and went to find a bottle of beer to wash away the foul taste lingering in his mouth.

Because of her request for alimony and child support, they had periodic court appearances in order to dictate how much and how often he had to provide money to Jolene. In spite of the initial anger that she would dare ask for so much, he knew deep down it was the right thing to do. And somehow sending money eased his conscience somewhat, as he figured at least he was playing a part in providing for their girls monetarily, since he wasn't there for them in person on a regular basis.

As he bided time in order to re-file for divorce, life took on a new normal. Not once did he consider the utter selfishness of his new lifestyle. He spent his days working before going home alone where he could smoke to his heart's content without any condemning glances or being banished to the barn. Weekends were one big party after another, only going home when he felt like it and without worry that anyone would be up waiting to lecture him or ask too many questions.

Tom's carelessness with money had been a frequent source of contention between him and Jolene, but her concern had served to keep him in check; at least a little. Now he was free to spend without restraint. Truth be told, all he really cared about was having enough cash in the bank to cover his alcohol consumption one weekend at a time.

One Friday evening, as he headed to the local tavern, he glanced inside his checkbook register: fifty dollars. Instead of being concerned how close he was cutting it, considering his next paycheck wouldn't be coming for a few days, he mentally figured how long that amount would last him in terms of alcohol. At the cost of two dollars a beer he figured he was good until Saturday night. So off he went and blew every cent.

Before long, the weekend binges were spilling over into his workweek. Many a night he would find himself at the bar, putting down a twelve pack, not leaving until the barkeeper said it was time to lock up. Once home, he would crash until time to head to work again at five a.m.

But it became increasingly difficult to pull himself out of bed after a night of drinking. Sometimes the only thing that helped get him going was another drink on his way to work. Or even on the job. He began to favor a concoction of vodka and cranberry juice, taking it with him in a thermos and sipping throughout the workday.

Numb to the danger in which he was placing himself and others as he drank and drove, he seemed oblivious to the fact his life was becoming more and more of a shipwreck. In rare sober moments, he was often shaken by the realization he couldn't remember how he had gotten home the night before. But he found any worry that surfaced was usually best taken care of by drowning it in yet another drink.

One particular night on the way home from an evening at the bar, Tom was abruptly brought to his senses by the jostling of his truck over unusually rough terrain. His shock as he realized he was driving 50 miles per hour in the middle of a cornfield momentarily sobered him up.

Questions raced to the forefront of his mind. How on earth had he gotten here? And how would he find his way out?

For a fleeting moment his conscience was sharpened enough to consider just how much he was destroying his life. More frightening yet was the thought he could very easily destroy someone else's in the process. What if he had just driven into the path of an oncoming car rather than a cornfield? But almost as quickly as the rational thought entered his brain, justification and thirst for alcohol beckoned and drowned it out. He told himself he just needed to get home, sleep this off and forget all about it.

At work there were days when it seemed to take him four hours to do a half hour job. He had left the corporate world shortly after he and Jolene had gone their separate ways. His current employer was a dear friend whose love for Christ enabled him to extend much more grace and mercy towards Tom than most ever would have considered doing. Instead of being grateful, Tom's mindset had become so self-centered he hardly realized all that his boss was doing for him or the awkward position in which his behavior consistently placed his employer.

In fact, the more he drank the less he cared about the feelings or condemnation of others. Worse yet, he was entirely numbed to the condemnation of his sin, which was separating him further and further from a holy God.

He no longer felt any conviction at all. He lived for the bottle and cared for little else. No matter where he went, a bottle usually went with him. Once when Jolene asked if he could meet her halfway between Forrest and Elgin, he agreed. But before leaving home that afternoon he filled a water bottle up with vodka, which he sipped throughout the trip. By the time he arrived in Morris his bottle was empty so he stopped at a liquor store, purchased more, and refilled his water bottle before meeting her at Culver's.

Having drunk too much already, when Jolene ordered a kid's meal he had belligerently remarked, "What are we, like two years old again?" He vaguely realized his voice must have dripped with more sarcasm than he intended when the guy behind the counter had shot him a questioning glance, obviously surprised by his rude behavior.

As soon as they sat at a table, Tom pulled out a legal pad to jot down notes from the conversation about to take place. But when he woke the next morning and looked at his notepad to jog his memory about whatever they had discussed, it was completely empty. He had been so trashed he hadn't bothered to write a single thing!

At work that day when his boss had asked how his meeting with Jolene had gone, Tom sarcastically replied, "I don't know. I was blacked out!"

In spite of his carefulness around the girls in the early days of their separation, with time he grew more and more lax on his custody weekends. Many times he was too tired to do anything but park them in front of the TV for hours on end.

Yet he truly treasured the time they spent together and often wished it wasn't so limited. Consequently, when his daughters whined or argued with one another, he chose to ignore it, not wanting to put them into a time out and waste even a few of their precious minutes at his house.

He was also quick to buy them anything they asked for, in a subconscious attempt to compensate for being apart so much of the time. Many weekends when he took them to meet Jolene he felt her disapproving glare as they climbed out of his truck with bags of new makeup, nail polish, or whatever else they'd cajoled him into buying for them. Never having been the "girly" type herself Jolene couldn't relate to or understand why they needed to get sucked into such frivolous things at their young ages. When she confronted him about it, and asked him to stop what she considered to be spoiling them, the irritation he felt towards her interference made him all the more determined to continue buying trinkets for them. She already had them disproportionately more of the time than he did. He had every right to bestow gifts on them in the few short hours they spent together each month!

He was determined she would not tell him how to parent. Even though in his heart of hearts he realized his parenting skills were leaving much to be desired, he did NOT need advice from her!

He might not be perfect but she obviously wasn't either!

If she were, they wouldn't be in the mess they were right now.

Chapter 10

For Jolene, being given a mandatory two-year waiting period before a judge would even consider Tom's second divorce filing was a welcome relief. She viewed it as a second chance. Or, more realistically, maybe this was the third, fourth, or even fifth chance to heal their damaged relationship! Regardless, she was thankful there was still time for them to work things out before divorce marked the legal end to their marriage.

Truth be told, many mornings when Jolene awoke she didn't necessarily have any desire to get back together with Tom. The break from their unhealthy communication patterns had proven to be a welcome respite in many ways. Watching his life deteriorate from afar was hard enough. She was thankful she wasn't being drug through it on a daily basis.

But divorce seemed so final! In spite of not being in a rush to get back together for the time being, she definitely desired to leave the door open for that possibility in the future. There were just many things she wanted to see Tom change first.

So the day their divorce was denied, she had left the courtroom with a deep sense of peace, realizing God was still in control. Perhaps Tom thought he could dispose of her, but ultimately it was God who would have the final say. If He chose to restore their broken marriage, she firmly believed He could and would.

Granted, there were rare occasions during their separation when Tom *did* raise her hopes with what seemed to be a change of heart. He would initiate a meeting, showing up full of assurances that he had truly changed and wanted to work things out.

Each time the pattern was the same: he would attempt to win her back by focusing on externals he thought would be impressive: shaving his goatee, quitting his smoking habit, putting on dress clothes and, for all practical purposes, outwardly appearing the part of the husband she'd always wanted him to be. But it rarely took long before something she said would upset him and she would once again see his true colors.

Undoubtedly, he was still the same Tom behind the clean-shaven exterior. He might have sincerely wanted her back, at least for the moment, but each time it quickly became obvious he wasn't ready to take Jesus back into his life yet. And without the redeeming power of Christ, his puny efforts at change failed time after time. As much as she desired to salvage their relationship in the long term, from a realistic viewpoint she knew it wasn't possible until Tom underwent a complete transformation. Although she never once believed divorce was the answer, neither was going back to the dysfunctional marriage they had experienced. Yes, her heart's desire was to be reunited...but not until they were ready to live together peaceably in a God-honoring relationship, demonstrating for their girls what a healthy marriage really should look like.

While she hoped and waited for that time, the emotional roller coaster of those failed attempts took its toll and continually fueled her frustration towards Tom.

She finally gave him an ultimatum: He didn't need to *tell* her he had changed ever again. She would *know* if he really did.

In the intervening months, they settled into the shared custody routine and Jolene adjusted to being a single mom throughout the week. Yet a growing uneasiness that something was creating a barrier between her and the Lord continued to fester and eat at her soul.

Finally, eighteen months after the denial of their divorce, things came to a head.

For quite awhile Jolene had been seeking advice from a godly counselor whom she highly esteemed. As he tried to help her work through all the pain of her circumstances, she was a dedicated and willing student. Soaking up the suggested activities, she worked hard to read and study the Scriptures he shared with her. But no matter what she read or how hard she studied, she couldn't seem to make real progress in healing.

Finally one day, blunt words spoken by her counselor brought Jolene to her senses like an ice-cold bucket of water in the face.

"You are turning into a bitter woman, Jo."

The words hung heavy in the air, stinging deeply as they sucked the breath out of her. In fact, the impact of his words hit with such incredible force, their impact seemed every bit as harsh to her ears as the words spoken by Tom when he admitted he had been unfaithful.

He had continued, "Jesus says you *have to* forgive. You don't see how this is tearing you down!"

Her first instinct was to defend herself, "But you just don't understand what all Tom put me through..." However, before the words were completely out of her mouth, she swallowed them with a difficult gulp.

Painful as it was, instead of a typical reaction of justifying the bitterness she harbored, this time she allowed the truth of what he had said to sink in. Sitting silently, she felt a chill as his stern warning worked its way through her entire being. With the precision of a laser beam, the truthful words shone into the dark corners of her heart, revealing and illuminating the sin hidden there.

Flesh and Spirit waged war within her. As difficult as it was to hear what he had to say, more painful still was the realization there really was no way she could refute his wise words.

Suddenly, in a moment of clarity, Jolene realized what had been choking out the intimacy in her relationship with her Savior. As the scales fell off her eyes, she finally saw clearly just how much she had allowed a root of bitterness to spring up in her heart. Once there, it had begun to spread lethal tendrils, squeezing the life out of her relationship with her Father.

Over the course of the next few days, Jolene could focus on little else, to the extent her preoccupation and introspection became evident to those around her. One afternoon as she was sitting by her parent's pool contemplating her counselor's words her brother broke into her thoughts, questioning what her counselor had said to upset her so much.

Praying before bed that night, Jolene recognized she had reached a crossroads. The choice was up to her but she was fully aware her decision would affect all those around her, especially her three daughters.

Would she choose to forgive?

Or would she continue to hold onto the hurt, nurse her wounds and cultivate resentment towards Tom?

One choice would lead her through what could prove to be a very painful and humbling soul searching, but the other was already choking her with the misery of bitterness.

In the end, the choice was obvious. It was time to swing wide the secret door of her heart!

Never before had Jolene realized the complexities of forgiveness. Now, under the guidance of her mentor, she studied what forgiveness really was. And also what it wasn't.

She quickly learned that forgiveness was not an easy choice, nor was it a simple one-time decision. Some days it was purely a moment-by-moment act of the will.

She also discovered forgiving Tom wasn't dependent upon reconciliation. Nor was it equal to *forgetting* the pain he had inflicted.

But probably most difficult of all was embracing the newly grasped concept that true forgiveness, in its simplest form, was merely *relinquishing her right to get even.*

Like most of humanity, her natural tendency was to seek revenge under the premise of "justice". Her flesh cried out that Tom needed to understand how severely he had wounded her and the girls...and then suffer in some way for the humiliation he had put her through.

One day as she was dwelling on her desire to "get even" she sensed the Lord laying something on her heart. "Jolene, you don't even know what to ask for in order to adequately punish Tom for what he's done." Then she was reminded of the latter part of the verse in Romans 12:19: "Beloved, do not avenge yourselves, but rather give place to wrath; for it is written, Vengeance is mine; I will repay, says the Lord."

It was a daily struggle, but Jolene ultimately came to terms with the fact it wasn't *her* responsibility to deal with what Tom had done. Nor was it her right to punish him in any way. God alone was justified in dealing with his soul.

Her advisor had shared some straightforward guidelines for sincere forgiveness:

I will no longer bring it up to Tom

I will no longer bring it up to myself

I will no longer bring it up to anybody else

I will not let it hinder my love

According to those principles, Jolene had new habits to learn.

First was deciding to let go of the record of wrongs she had been keeping in her own mind. Without realizing it, she had grown accustomed to mentally rehearsing the continually growing list of Tom's infractions against her. Doing so usually led to feeling justified in holding a grudge against him or, worse yet, finding not-so-subtle ways to remind him of his mistakes.

Instead, she now learned she had to lay it all down. Privately, before God.

For months, years even, she had sought comfort by venting their problems to her family, friends, and previous counselors, soaking up their sympathy like salve on an open wound. Now, she was becoming aware just how lethal this seemingly harmless habit had been to their relationship. Whenever she was tempted to air Tom's latest infraction out loud, she had to consciously remind herself to take the high road of forgiveness instead. Inevitably, she would find herself on her knees laying the grievance down at her Father's feet, entrusting Him to deal with it in His great wisdom and perfect timing rather than any feeble attempts at justice on her own.

Although it hadn't ever been a conscience decision, she now realized she had subconsciously been withholding forgiveness from Tom as a means of punishing him for all the pain he had inflicted.

Sure, she had been willing and ready to forgive, *if* and *when* he would come with a truly repentant heart and humbly ask her to.

Of course, since *that* had never happened, she hadn't felt obligated to grant forgiveness either.

Now she learned she needed to forgive him regardless of whether he ever asked or even acknowledged his need for her forgiveness.

Choosing to forgive proved to be a slow, painful process but eventually, her eyes were opened to a surprising reality. By attempting to lock Tom in chains *she* had become the real prisoner, bound by shackles of unforgiveness harbored in her own heart.

Soon she discovered a beautiful truth; the more she released her grudges against Tom, the freer *she* became. In fact, by working to loosen *his* bonds, she was actually liberating *herself*!

She also discovered each choice to forgive Tom brought about further healing in her heart.

And step-by-step, the intimacy between her and the LORD was being restored.

Chapter 11

*N*ot far into Jolene's journey towards forgiveness, the mandatory two-year waiting period ended.

It came as no surprise when Tom promptly filed a second time for divorce.

Throughout the hearings the first time, and once again after he filed the second time, Jolene made sure to ask him the same question each time they had to meet in court. "Are you sure you want to go through with this?"

The irony had never been lost on her. How odd that *she* would continually ask *him* to rethink divorce. Wasn't *she* the victim here? *He* had been the unfaithful one. *He* should be groveling at her feet, asking for forgiveness and begging *her* to give him one more chance to work it out. Even the judge had agreed she wasn't guilty of mental cruelty.

So why was *she* still the one trying to save their lifeless marriage from completely dying?

Because no matter how ludicrous it seemed, even when their situation looked virtually impossible from a human perspective, she held onto the belief that they would get back together. Someday.

So, at their final court appearance, while waiting in the hallway for their case to be called, Tom steeled himself for the dreaded question.

Once again, she didn't disappoint. Calm and matter-of-fact, as if discussing a simple business transaction, Jolene approached him and questioned if this was really what he wanted to do.

Frustration coursed through his being. Instead of causing him to reconsider his actions her question only served to strengthen his resolve. Even now, after years of separation and just minutes prior to their divorce, he felt his authority being undermined by her.

Hadn't it always been that way, with her second-guessing his decisions? He reminded himself that this was one of his main reasons for desiring to be divorced from this woman.

"Of course this is what I want to do!" he brusquely assured her and then turned away to redirect his attention to his attorney.

Shortly afterwards, Jolene and her lawyer entered the courtroom and went over their part of the settlement and what she would be asking for. Next Tom and his lawyer joined them and worked out the minor details. Thankfully, they were able to come to an agreement fairly easily on all but the cost of the girls' health insurance premiums. Because the four of them were unable to work out a reasonable solution, the judge was eventually called in to her chair. After looking at both of their incomes, she made a ruling for them to split the premium equally; a big win in Tom's favor.

With that, they all signed the divorce judgment and copies were made.

It had taken multiple hearings, piles of paperwork, and exorbitant attorney fees, but that day Tom finally won his case.

Eight years prior, on February 2, 1997, in front of a cloud of friends and family gathered as witnesses, Tom and Jolene Young had spoken vows to stay united until parted by death. Now, on May 6, 2005, in a quiet courtroom with two attorneys and a judge, in less than an hour's time, their marriage had been declared legally dead with the bang of a judge's gavel.

"Irreconcilable Differences."

For Tom, there was great satisfaction in the court's decision. He believed their marriage had died long ago. For all practical purposes, he had checked out of the relationship two years prior in that very same courthouse. But today he felt he had finally trumped Jolene and won. In his eyes, the insurance ruling had simply been icing on the cake.

As he walked outside to his car that bright spring day, Tom felt what he believed to be true freedom at last. Legally declared free from the responsibility of being a husband to Jolene Young meant he no longer had to hear her gripe. She would no longer have any control over his life or expect him to meet certain criteria that seemed unattainable to him.

For Jolene that day in court proved to be a major turning point.

Until the divorce was finalized she had constantly felt the need to cling to her faith that their marriage would somehow be restored someday and had felt it her duty to remain open to salvaging it, regardless of her feelings. .

But once the gavel came down, she subconsciously washed her hands of Tom and their marriage.

In her mind, it was now completely over; she had done what she could and it was time to move on and put the past behind.

Because God had not chosen to work a miracle in her marriage, she held to the assumption that He had another plan in mind.

Four months after the divorce, the door opened for Jolene and the girls to purchase a house two miles from her parent's. With the help of family, she began fixing the home up, making it a cozy refuge for Shelby, Shania, and Shayna. It was a relief to have their own space again and she found it satisfying to be providing as well as she was for herself and the girls with min-imal financial help from Tom.

This proved to be a time of emotional stability and an abiding calm for Jolene. She took great comfort in knowing God had deemed her strong enough to endure the trials that had come her way, including the challenges of being a single mom.

Yet she was all too aware He had also deemed her weak enough that He had been forced to allow drastic measures to get her attention and teach her to fully depend on Him.

And depend on Him she did!

Through the difficult moments of single parenting, she truly learned to lean into Christ, knowing He would never leave or let her down like Tom had done.

Interestingly, as they each went about the process of moving on in their own way neither Tom nor Jolene ever imagined get-ting married to someone else.

Jolene's decision was based on her interpretation of Scripture regarding marriage, divorce, and remarriage. God had created the institution of marriage in the Garden of Eden and ordained it to be a picture in the flesh of the relationship between Christ and the Church. Therefore it was easy to see that from His per-spective, marriage was a sacred relationship of divine signifi-cance and not one to be taken lightly.

Although she was aware that current Christian culture had grown increasingly accepting of divorce and remarriage, from her search of the Bible she didn't believe remarriage was an option she could or would consider. In fact, she firmly believed in God's eyes she and Tom were still married. According to Roman 7:1-3, she was bound to Tom and would only be released from the law that bound them if he should die.

Ashamed to admit it, Jolene had allowed herself the luxury of considering that possibility from time to time. During a short period of hopelessness early on in their separation she had been tempted by Satan to imagine what life could be like if something were to happen to Tom, releasing her from her vows to him. Though she had been wracked with guilt afterwards for the morbid thoughts, there had been a few days when she had dreamed of being free to remarry someone who would truly love and cherish her; someone who would prove to be the kind of husband and father she had always envisioned.

One night, however, she had felt the Lord speaking to her from St. John 18:11 where Jesus, upon being betrayed by Judas, commanded Peter to put his sword away. Christ assured Peter it wasn't necessary to defend Him with violence there in the Garden of Gethsemane because He knew He needed to drink the cup that His Father had asked of Him. Jolene was deeply convicted by the Scripture. If Jesus willingly accepted His "cup" (the trial of the cross) she should be willing to do no less than accept the much smaller trial He had asked her to bear. Pathetic as it may be compared to the cross Christ had borne, it seemed her "cross" for the time being was her wedding vow to Tom, divorced or not. If God was asking her to bear this cross she felt the necessity to do so willingly, sticking it out to the end. What gave her the greatest courage and comfort was the knowledge that the Lord intimately understood her heart, thoughts and intentions. She could trust that He knew her well enough to know if this trial was what was best for her in the long run.

In light of that, she was fully convicted that the vows the two of them had taken in front of God were binding in the Heavenly courtroom and no legal decision in an earthly court of law could ever alter that relationship. However, she didn't expect Tom to hold the same conviction, since he no longer cared two hoots about God's laws or walking in obedience to them.

In fact, one day while they had been arguing on the phone about some issue, Tom had finally blurted out unfeelingly, "Why don't you just go get married to someone else and leave me alone, Jolene?" His harsh words had made her wonder if he was perhaps considering remarriage himself.

However, in spite of his obvious disregard for the Word, Jolene had shared her convictions with him early on in the divorce, reminding him of God's admonition in Deuteronomy 24:1–4 and how it related to them. If Tom were ever to marry someone else and then divorce that wife, Jolene told him she would never feel free to marry him again.

Unknown to her, that warning had haunted Tom. Taking up residence in his subconscious mind, the thought prevented him from ever seriously considering marriage as an option in spite of the various relationships in which he found himself. Granted, it wasn't out of a desire to honor God, but more out of his fear that doing so would forever jeopardize any hopes of a future relationship with Jolene, should he ever decide he wanted her back.

The fact that his thought process was motivated by pure selfishness never once crossed his mind. Perhaps because selfishness had taken a hold of their marriage and been steering the relationship for so long it was just second nature at that point. Ultimately, for him it was all about having his way. The harsh, ugly truth was, even after the divorce initiated by him, deep down inside he still wanted to be sure she was available, just in case he ever changed his mind.

Although he wouldn't have admitted it to a single soul, illogical as it was, he still thought of Jolene. Frequently, in fact.

After his relationship with the woman from work ended Tom had gone on to date other women from time to time throughout their separation and divorce, yet he still found his thoughts consistently turning towards Jolene at the strangest times. Sometimes even in the presence of a girlfriend, he would find his mind wasn't on his date but on his ex-wife. The old adage, "Can't live with her, can't live without her" definitely held true for him in his feelings towards the woman he'd married and subsequently divorced.

At one point not long after the divorce was final, Tom reached a low point. Even though he had initially been jubilant by the official dissolution of their marriage, suddenly he was consumed with wanting Jolene back. He found himself crying almost continuously, desperately desiring to have her in the truck beside him instead of the woman who sat there right then.

But the chasm between them seemed too deep and too wide to cross anymore. He was aware Jolene was growing closer to Jesus while he was running fast and furiously in the opposite direction.

It made no sense anyway. Why would he want to go back to the way things had been with her? Yet he couldn't shake the loneliness or his longing for what he'd given up. So he sought to numb his emotions the only way he knew how. But sometimes the alcohol only served to magnify his feelings.

With time, Tom's perspective shifted. In the heat of the battles during marriage and while he'd been pursuing divorce, his focus had always centered on the negatives about Jolene and their relationship.

He'd firmly believed the bad outweighed the good.

But the longer they were apart and, with time serving as the ultimate healer of wounds, Tom began to recall the laughter they'd shared, memories they'd made, and moments when marriage actually *had* been good.

A new question began to haunt him day and night; why had they given up what they had?

Sure, they had experienced their fair share of conflict, without a doubt. He'd even managed to convince a judge their differences were beyond the realm of reconciliation! But now he wondered if they'd really tried hard enough. Sometimes he couldn't help but wonder if things would have turned out differently if they had gone to counseling earlier. They had attempted various "counselors" throughout their marriage, but unfortunately they had been untrained, ministerial counselors who hadn't understood the depth of their issues or been adequately equipped to deal with problems of their magnitude. By the time they finally ended up in a professional's office it was a little too late. Even though everything the man had said made perfect sense and deeply resonated with Tom, at the time he had already decided he was through trying.

There was nothing he could do about it now, anyway. It was what it was.

But one night after dropping his date off at her house Tom trudged back to his truck with a hollow ache deep inside.

Suddenly an odd question popped into his mind. "If I were dying in a hospital, who would I want at my side?"

The immediate answer, without any hesitation whatsoever, was "Jolene!"

More questions raced through his head.

So why had they let their marriage die? Why wasn't he with *her* tonight? What were she and the girls doing right now?

A symphony of regrets began playing in his head with accusations of, "If only..." keeping rhythm to the relentless beat.

That's when Satan pounced on him with a vicious reminder: "You were never good enough, Tom! Remember? You could never measure up to her expectations." He had to agree. Hadn't that been the problem? He had never been good enough for Jolene before; why would he think it could be any different now?

That night, instead of driving straight home from his girlfriend's house, he found himself pulling into the bar. Checking his watch, he saw he had forty-five minutes until closing time. Walking inside, he ordered a drink and hoped this time it would drown out the voices in his head and the gnawing ache in his heart for his ex-wife and their three darling daughters.

But when he crawled into bed an hour and a half later, he had to admit defeat.

Again.

Would these feelings ever end?

Second Wedding (October 18, 2008)

Tom & Jolene: Still in Love (August 2014)

Tom & Jolene's Three Princesses: Shayna, Shelby, Shania (August 2014)

A Very Thankful Family (August 2014)

Chapter 12

There had been many severe blows to Tom and Jolene's relationship over the years but without a doubt his affair was what had ultimately pushed them towards the breaking point. Because of the havoc wreaked on his family by his indiscretion, Tom had committed to himself he would never again betray another individual by being romantically involved with more than one woman simultaneously.

But selfish living leads to lack of self control and suddenly he found himself being sucked in by Satan. Instead of actively resisting, he just went along for the ride until, about one and a half years after his divorce, he found himself dating multiple women at the same time.

Once again his unfaithfulness had caused him to plunge to the very depths to which he'd vowed he would never sink.

When he realized just how low he'd allowed himself to sink, he fell to his knees, dropping his head on the ground in despair.

A wail from somewhere deep inside fought its way to the surface. He didn't know how long he lay in that position, trembling, as sob after sob engulfed him and wracked his entire body.

Eventually the wailing turned to desperate moans of a miserable man whose heart is full of regret and remorse.

Finally, without even considering the weight or impact of what was coming from his own lips, the groaning of Tom's heart took the form of repentant words spoken out loud, confessing his deplorable state.

"I'm so sick and tired of living this life, God! I am such a miserable sinner. Jesus, I need your help!" The words poured out of him in a rush. He continued emotionally, *"I can't do this on my own. Help me, Jesus! I need you!"*

And there, in the midst of all the stench of his filth and sin, the Savior came and met him!

As the brilliance of Jesus' holiness illuminated every sinful thought and action in Tom's life, he nearly felt crushed under the burden of it all. The price for a sinner like him was just too great to pay. How could he ever match up to the holiness of the Savior standing before him? He knew what a filthy, wretched person he had become; he would never be good enough to deserve forgiveness for all he had done!

That's when *grace* stepped in.

Before the weight of his transgressions utterly destroyed him, Tom was reminded of a beautiful truth from Romans 5:8,

"But God demonstrates His own love toward us, in that, while we were yet sinners, Christ died for us." Embracing that truth meant he didn't have to be clean to come to Jesus; Jesus would take him just as he was...and make him clean!

And that is exactly what the Savior did! Right then and there, as Tom placed his faith in the cleansing power of Jesus' blood, his sins were washed away by the perfect, sinless blood of the Lamb. The great chasm of sin that had separated Tom from his Savior for so long had finally been spanned by a simple, repentant prayer!

Throughout his life Tom had attempted many times in various ways to erect his own bridge of self-righteousness and good works, but had always failed miserably. Now he understood why. Man was never meant to build a bridge to Christ. Rather, Christ had already built a perfectly simple bridge to mankind...in the form of an old rugged cross!

As soon as he confessed his deep sinfulness and need of salvation, Tom had felt the very real presence of Jesus entering his heart. He also sensed another very real, very dark presence in the room; without a doubt, a spiritual battle was being waged for his soul. Kneeling by his bed, the feeling of evil was so tangible he found himself glancing over his shoulder to see if there was actually someone, or something, in the room with him.

Suddenly afraid of the dark, Tom went to sleep with the hallway and bathroom lights brightly burning that night. He sensed a spiritual tension around him, and had the distinct impression someone was being kicked out of his home...and that someone was very unhappy, indeed!

Unfortunately, the battle didn't end that night. Most enemies don't surrender easily, and Satan is definitely no exception. His attacks against Tom were ruthless.

Intellectually, Tom knew God had forgiven him, but with the enemy of his soul continually whispering accusations in his ear, he had a difficult time accepting the truth of his forgiveness all the way down into his heart. Instead of walking in peace, he continued to do battle with feelings of shame and guilt that he just couldn't shake.

The only weapon at such times is the Sword of the Spirit; the Word of God. Tom began earnestly seeking comfort in the Bible and arming himself with ammunition to wield against the lies of Satan.

Instead of drinking binges until the wee hours of morning he now found himself staying home to pour over the Bible. Even though he had spent years as a "Christian" he had never before immersed himself in Scripture, devouring each verse, like he did now. He clung to every word like a dying man in a desert stumbling upon a life-giving spring of water.

His prayers took on new meaning, too.

Before, he had directed his prayers to God in a formal manner, out of duty and habit. Suddenly he was praying to God not only as his Savior but also a personal Friend, Companion, and Helper.

He began to lay his life at Jesus' feet, begging Him to change whatever He felt needed to be changed. Instead of making the *outside* "clean" like he had tried to do over and over again in the past, now Tom simply asked Jesus to begin a total transformation from the *inside out*.

Then he patiently waited on the Lord to bring conviction to his heart. He was determined his motives be pure, with everything done for Jesus and not praise of men. No more arrogant pride on his part, no trying to earn the Lord's favor, or walking in fear of man's expectations. He truly wanted to be who *Jesus* asked him to be.

Nothing more, nothing less.

Right in the beginning Tom kept his newfound intimacy with Jesus to himself. He clearly remembered Jolene's admonishment, "When you change you won't have to tell me. I will be able to see for myself." He decided to put it to the test not just with her, but with others he came in contact with.

It didn't take long.

In contrast to the way he used to live, attempting to portray being a Christian through his own actions, self-denials, and lifestyle, he now learned to relax and let the light of Jesus shine brightly from within, recognizing the God of the Universe was big enough to speak for Himself.

One day he showed up for a blood draw at a clinic where he had become a familiar face over the years. The nurse who had grown accustomed to seeing Tom took one look at him and questioned, "What's different about you today?" Although at this point he had not felt conviction to change outwardly, the radiant love of Jesus was bringing about a transformation that couldn't help but be noticed! In the process, He was able to point all glory to God rather than accept praise for any efforts on his part.

Upon breaking off the relationships he had been pursuing with worldly women in exchange for his pursuit of Christ, Tom began to struggle with a new issue. Suddenly he found himself fighting such a deep repulsion for females it bordered on the verge of hatred.

He hated the immodesty he saw all around him; immodesty that he knew had played a part in his caving to temptation. He was angry about *what* had happened and *why* it had happened.

Spending his evenings at home reading God's Word, Tom decided to study the entire story of shepherd-turned-king David in I & II Samuel, I Kings, and the Psalms. Making a list of all the recorded times David sinned and was forgiven, he noticed a pattern emerging: David got caught, he confessed, recognized and accepted the consequences, and then the forgiveness came.

The truth of the matter was that God is always willing and able to pardon sin. But excuses can never be forgiven.

As that reality settled over him, he was slammed by conviction. How many times had he made excuses for his behavior; accusing Jolene, her parents, her friends, church, and even God, for his actions?

Eventually, the Spirit opened his eyes further. Even his current attitude of anger towards all women was an attempt to excuse his own behavior by shifting the blame. If he wanted full forgiveness, it was time to truthfully own up to his own sinfulness rather than point fingers at anyone else. Laying every transgression before his Father, one by one, he was able to begin embracing the amazing truth that there is *no* sin beyond the scope of God's forgiveness.

At the same time he came to grips with the distressing reality that some sins, though forgiven, leave scars that last a lifetime. Studying more of King David's life, the concept of the costliness of sin became obvious. Though David was forgiven for his sin with Bathsheba, God still allowed him to reap harsh consequences through the death of their beloved child. The truth of the matter is that *sin always costs someone something!*

With the scales of selfishness finally removed from his eyes, the price tag that Satan had so craftily hidden from his view suddenly came clearly into focus. It was plain to see his selfishness had come at a cost way beyond what he had ever imagined or understood.

Tom had lived with regret for far too long, but now remorse hit him in waves.

Not only had he wounded Jolene, he finally admitted to himself how deeply his actions had also wounded his extended family and friends. But most of all, his girls. Although completely innocent in the whole mess, they had suffered incredibly because of choices *he* had made.

Eventually he came to terms with the realization what he had put them through would be a deep regret he would simply have to live with the rest of his life. Nonetheless, shouldering responsibility and admitting blame on his part would go a long way in the healing process of the girls' tender hearts, as well as his own.

Although Tom was growing immeasurably in his walk with the Lord and believed he was fully forgiven by God, he struggled daily to view himself as worthy of being fully pardoned by the Savior of the world. To help him along in the process of forgiving himself, he finally sought out professional help from a wise counselor who quickly developed into a true mentor and friend. As they worked through the process together, Tom began to fully embrace all that forgiveness meant and how to accept the unfathomable pardon of Christ, even though it wasn't easy.

With time he came to understand his counselor's statement, "God forgave you long before you forgave yourself!"

Eventually, Tom invited Jolene to attend an appointment with him, hopeful that a joint session could prove beneficial to both of them.

Her reply, however, had been kind but firm.

"No thanks. I care about you as a person but I no longer love you as a husband. I'm happy with where I am now."

Uncharacteristically, Tom felt no anger at her response. By now he had matured to the point of being willing to take full responsibility for his sin and was able to respect her decision. He understood that, in spite of being forgiven by God, he was reaping what he'd sowed just as King David so often had.

Although he couldn't bring himself to entirely give up hope Jolene would change her mind, he determined from that point on to focus on running hard after Jesus, loving *Him* first and foremost. Because his chances of getting Jolene back seemed fairly slim from a human perspective, Tom decided to put all his heart into becoming the man God asked him to be. Yet he would continue to do everything in his power to reconcile with Jolene to whatever extent God had planned.

Ultimately, he could rest in knowing God was in full control of both their lives; a fact which brought him deep peace and comfort.

Through the ongoing help of his counselor, Ron, and hours spent in quiet communion with God, Tom eventually came to a place where his security stemmed from Christ alone.

One day as he woke with the simple words of the old hymn, "Amazing Grace" ringing in his mind, he realized that he was not simply surviving life anymore; he was truly thriving!

Contemplating the unexpected emotion filling his heart with joy it became clear that his happiness was no longer based on Jolene, or anyone else for that matter. He wasn't bound by other's opinions or disapproval any more. Instead, he was filled with a deep abiding joy; a joy that came from being forgiven and loved by Jesus.

Amazing Grace, how sweet the sound,

That saved a wretch like me.

I once was lost but now am found,

Was blind, but now, I see.

Those words, simple as they were, spoke volumes. For so many years he truly had been blinded to how empty his life had been. In the midst of it he hadn't even recognized his desperate searching for what it was. But now as he contemplated how lost he had been and how Jesus had found him, Tom rejoiced with a sudden awareness:

His nagging emptiness had finally been filled!

What his heart had longed for all along had been Jesus!

Although God created him with a desire for human companionship, it had never been fair to expect Jolene to meet his every need. God never intended a wife to be all-sufficient for her husband, and vice versa.

Tom was beginning to grasp the age old truth that the deepest longings and most intimate places of every heart belong to Christ alone.

Before, he had only given pieces of his heart to the Lord; now he held nothing back. With Jesus becoming his One and Only, Tom was developing a relationship with the Savior far beyond anything he had ever imagined.

And for now, that was enough.

Chapter 13

As weeks passed, Jolene began to wonder if this "new" Tom just might be for real. She couldn't help but be impressed with the consistency she observed in his behavior whenever they met to swap the girls or had reason to communicate on the phone. He even began showing up occasionally at her church on his non-custody weekends, driving two hours each way, just in order to spend more time with Shelby, Shania, and Shayna. It hadn't escaped Jolene's notice he seemed to be making a valiant attempt at respecting her feelings, carefully communicating his plans ahead of time so she wasn't taken by surprise during any of his visits. This was in stark contrast to previous days when he had shown up unexpectedly a few times at school or church functions, even daring to drag a girlfriend along once or twice. Each of those incidents had given Jolene the impression he was intentionally invading "her" territory, which infuriated her.

But over the course of time, Jolene had discovered a life of peace-filled contentment for herself and her three daughters. Although being a single mom was not an ideal situation, nor one she would have ever chosen for herself, she was confident God had used the pain of her circumstances to refine and shape her into a vessel more useful to Him.

Without a husband she had been forced to learn a life of full dependence on Jesus as her Bridegroom. So much so that the thought of going back to Tom now raised concerns in her mind about how to deal with what would undoubtedly be competing loyalty in her life.

Regardless, she had an unspoken timeframe in mind in which to test this "new and improved" version of Tom. Unsure how or why she had come to the decision, she inwardly held to a belief that Tom needed to prove himself to her for at least five years before she would even begin to consider any form of reconciliation.

So for now they went on living their separate lives.

Still, Tom continued to ask her periodically to attend counseling with him. In response, she continued to politely reject the offers. Finally, during one of his visits to Elgin, some men from her congregation offhandedly commented how settled and happy Jolene seemed to be. It wasn't said in a spiteful way and Tom was truly appreciative of their honesty. In fact, he was comforted by the knowledge God had helped Jolene heal to the point where others could witness a contented spirit in her; something he had longed to see in his wife throughout their marriage.

That day he decided it was time to let go of his desire to have her attend counseling with him. As much as he struggled with the idea, he also had to wonder if the time had come for him to accept the very real possibility he might never be reconciled to Jolene.

It was a difficult journey for Tom, forcing him to come face to face with the deepest longings of his heart and the impact they had on his faith in God. Being perfectly honest with himself, he had to admit just how much he still hoped to win Jolene back.

The account of Abraham and Isaac in Genesis 22 held profound lessons for Tom. In this Scripture it is apparent God didn't really need—or even want—Isaac's life as a sacrifice. What He truly desired was the assurance Abraham's heart was completely devoted to Him; so devoted that he would sacrifice his precious son if that was what the LORD asked of him. Sometimes God still asks His people to surrender their most prized possession or relinquish the person dearest to them for His sake. He has the right to do so; it is His prerogative both to give and to take away. Nonetheless, the questions hit Tom in the pit of the stomach. Was he truly willing to relinquish everything and *everyone* for the sake of Christ? Would he continue to worship and love God, even if he were asked to lay Jolene down, never to receive her back?

In Genesis, as soon as Abraham proved he was willing to slay his son for God, a substitute lamb was provided. We still serve the same God, whose name is Jehovah-Jireh: God provides. Tom ultimately had to rest in that knowledge. If God asked him to relinquish his dreams and plans regarding Jolene, he would have to trust Jehovah-Jireh to live up to His name.

Only a week or two after Tom had decided to turn his desire for Jolene completely over to God, his counselor happened to visit her congregation. That day Jolene was able to speak with Ron and almost immediately asked his opinion regarding the authenticity of her ex-husband's changed heart.

In response, Ron encouraged her to come to a joint session with Tom. He kindly assured her it would provide an opportunity to ask questions, work through some of the issues in the presence of a third party, and maybe find a measure of healing for the pain they had inflicted upon each other during their troubled marriage.

What sealed the deal was his reassurance, "Even if there's no possibility of reconciliation, you'll at least have closure." Those words removed the pressure and provided a sense of relief. If she were to agree to attend a session, it clearly wouldn't be with the intent of getting back together; the purpose was simply to talk through their hurts in a controlled environment.

She considered and prayed for about a month before working up the courage to call Tom.

Purposefully keeping the conversation business-like, she immediately cut to the chase before she changed her mind about what she was about to say.

"I talked to Ron awhile back and he invited me to join you in a counseling session." Determined not to give him the wrong idea, she rushed on, "This is not a reconciling meeting. We can just see where the two of us are. Would that be ok?"

Expecting Tom to respond immediately in a positive manner, Jolene was taken aback by several seconds of awkward silence on the line.

Finally, with more than a hint of hesitation in his voice, he agreed to the idea and informed her he would call Ron with the news.

As she clicked off the phone, she exhaled and wondered what she'd just gotten herself into.

On the other end of the phone line, Tom was baffled by his own reaction. It hadn't been that long ago he had invited Jolene to attend with him and had been inwardly disappointed when she'd turned him down. So why had there been hesitation on his part today when she had not only agreed, but had actually taken the initiative upon herself? Admittedly, the Lord's timing confused him. Why was she willing now, just when he had begun to work through the possibility of never getting back together with her? Was he going to get his hopes up again, only to have them dashed once more?

Prone to analyzing, Tom realized his hesitation also stemmed from a place of fear and maybe even a strange sense of possessiveness. Through the months he had developed such a strong friendship with Ron that he wasn't sure he was ready to share the relationship with Jolene. During counseling sessions he felt understood, forgiven and appreciated. He wondered if including Jolene might destroy the peaceful place he'd found?

Finally, he turned to prayer. It didn't take the Holy Spirit long to speak conviction to his heart. "If there is even the slightest hope of reconciliation, you cannot close this door on her."

So, laying aside his concerns, he called Ron's office and confirmed a joint appointment for the two of them on the evening of October 16, 2007.

None knew what to expect as the three of them first sat down together in Ron's office. After all the pain of the past, including almost five years of separation, where would they even begin?

Ron opened with a prayer, inviting the Lord into their time together, before beginning to carefully guide the conversation.

During their meeting he asked both of them the same three questions:

Where are you in your life right now?

In your mind, is there any hope for your relationship?

Do you want your relationship with one another to grow?

Jolene not only acknowledged how happy and content she was, she also shared just how much God had helped her thrive as a single mom. And she adamantly declared she wasn't in the least bit anxious to see their relationship grow from where it currently stood. The thought of being hurt again scared her too much. In spite of that, the main point Tom heard and clung to was her answer to the second question; "Where there is life, there is hope".

Dare he begin to dream again of the possibility?

Throughout their session, Ron's calm presence, coupled with the spiritual maturity that had taken place in both Tom and Jolene since their marriage had fallen apart, allowed them to have a peaceful meeting in spite of the sensitivity of the subjects they discussed while the minutes quickly ticked away.

Near the end of their time, Ron looked at both of them and recommended giving the Lord six months to work in their relationship and reveal His plans for their future.

His words stirred deep frustration and irritation within Jolene. Was he really inferring six short months would be sufficient time to figure out if she wanted to reconcile with this man who had carelessly trampled her heart?

No matter how much Tom seemed to have changed, she was still determined he needed to prove himself to be faithful and true for at least five years before there was even anything to consider!

Jolene didn't let on in the meeting just how frustrated she felt but as she climbed into her vehicle for the three-hour drive back home, she was inwardly wound up in knots. Heading out into the dark countryside, she finally relaxed her grip on the steering wheel ever so slightly. Thoughts continued to tumble around in her mind as she replayed the conversation in Ron's office, especially the final comment.

The more she considered it, the more incredulous she became. *Six months!*

Glancing up at the clear October night sky, she half-heartedly noticed the brilliance of the twinkling lights above her.

Suddenly, a dazzling white star streaked across the sky right in front of her, leaving a sparkling trail behind. Her breath caught in her throat at the beauty of the sight. Shortly after, another falling star glittered its way across the heavens before burning out high above the earth.

In what would be a clear, defining moment in her life it was almost as if she heard her Father's voice speaking audibly to her from the passenger seat.

"Jo, when you first sought direction about marrying Tom I answered in one week. I think I can give you direction in six months. Let Me handle this!"

With those words, a sense of abiding calm rained down upon her. She felt the peace of God enfold her like a blanket. It was true; He was in control of everything; the stars, the sky, Tom's heart, her future. None of it was too big for Him to handle. All she needed to do was trust Him!

In awe that He would go to such great lengths to reassure and comfort her, she was once again convinced Jesus was working on her behalf and that He would never leave or forsake her.

She didn't have to figure out the future.

Her Father already had it all taken care of.

Chapter 14

Throughout that following week as she considered the conversation in Ron's office, Jolene came up with a list of questions she wanted to ask. So by the end of the week she called Tom again to request another joint session.

From there, one appointment led to another.

And then another.

After five appointments they decided one hour was hardly sufficient to cover all the questions and issues raised during their time together. So they decided to begin scheduling two hour sessions each month.

Even then the hands on the clock literally seemed to fly.

At one of their earliest appointments, Jolene had clearly restated she had no interest in remarriage to Tom. That part of their life was behind them and she was just trying to find resolution to all that had gone wrong. To her, reconciliation seemed too much of a risk to even consider at this point. But when she voiced that sentiment to Ron he related taking a risk to the principle of investing. In order to get a bigger and better return, a bigger risk is sometimes necessary. He encouraged her to at least pray for the courage to be willing to do so, if that was what God had planned.

That evening before bed she had opened her Bible to Ecclesiastes 11. There, in God's sovereign way, He lovingly reminded her through His Holy Word that life often involves both risk and opportunity. The Life Application notes in her Bible drove home the point with an admonition to pray for a spirit of faith and adventure instead of limiting God through fear or waiting for perfect conditions before taking a bold step forward.

She was convicted, realizing that's what her idea of a five-year timeframe to test Tom's behavior really boiled down to. Basically, she was saying she wasn't willing to take any risk until he proved to her "conditions were perfect".

Yet realistically, with two humans involved, perfection wasn't even attainable.

As she closed her journal and turned off the light, she prayed for the kind of faith her Bible spoke of as well as the courage Ron had called her to. But her heart wasn't truly ready to embrace either quite yet. Even as she spoke the words, she was all too aware she didn't honestly desire God to answer them.

Not now, at least.

However, from experience, she knew that sometimes it was necessary to ask God for that which she was not yet ready to receive. Sometimes He softens a heart through the discipline of continual asking. In time, His child becomes receptive to what He knew all along would be for their best. So, though it was perhaps not truly heartfelt, she began to consistently ask for courage and faith, trusting God to change the desire of her heart if it was His will.

Realizing the details might not be as extreme as Jolene was imagining, and hoping it would be a positive step towards rebuilding trust, Ron encouraged Tom during one session to give full disclosure of his sins since their marriage had dissolved.

Tom hung his head in shame, but after several deep breaths began to pour out his heart with great remorse, holding nothing back.

When he finished, every bone in his body ached as if he'd just run a marathon. He felt totally beat up, worn out and exhausted.

At the same time, he experienced a great release from finally having everything out in the open. No longer hiding behind any excuses, he had completely bared his soul and admitted all the deeds done in darkness.

Even though he knew he'd been forgiven by God months ago and his sins had been washed away by the crimson blood of Christ, he had continued to struggle regularly under the weight of his own condemning thoughts. But now that he had brought his sin into the light, he had confidence Satan's whispered accusations could no longer take root and bind him as they so often had in the past.

In spite of being so weary he could barely hold his head up, he needed to consider Jolene's heart and how deeply his confession might have wounded her.

For a split second his mind went back five years to their garage in Forrest when he'd admitted his affair for the first time. In those moments he had been completely self-absorbed, with very little remorse. Not caring how deeply his words wounded her, he had spitefully relished inflicting pain on her in return for the years of unhappiness he'd been forced to endure throughout their marriage.

In stark contrast, here in the cozy office of his counselor, Tom's own feelings were almost immediately overshadowed by his deep concern for his ex-wife.

Slowly lifting his eyes to meet hers, he dreaded the pain he was certain to find reflected there. Curiously, though the pain he expected to witness was indeed evident, he also observed apprehension and even confusion mingled together in her expression.

In truth, Jolene had been somewhat surprised as she'd sat quietly listening. Based on the path he had been heading down while they were still married, she had envisioned him living a life of much deeper depravity than what he had described.

So when his voice had drifted off and he'd raised his head to glance her way she silently waited, expecting him to finish. When it was apparent he was through speaking, she struggled to believe he had been completely honest. She couldn't help wondering how much he had withheld.

Not that he'd portrayed a life free from sin or Christ-honoring by any stretch of the imagination. But, assuming the worst, she had definitely expected far more than what he'd shared.

As they left the office shortly after, Tom was so washed out from the experience he couldn't even muster the strength to hold the door open for Jolene. Walking out together, she was uncharacteristically quiet as she mulled it all over; a radical change in behavior that did not go unnoticed by either of them.

They both recalled full well that during their years as husband and wife, Jolene had rarely backed down until she had addressed and spoken her mind on a matter. Too many times to count Tom had accused her of being a nagger. In contrast, his gut reaction in conflict had always been to withdraw, either to the barn, chicken coops or to check on the ducklings they raised in swimming pools.

The vast differences in their communication styles had consistently widened the gulf and raised the tension between them. Rarely, if ever, did their attempts at conflict resolution bring the peace they desperately sought.

Through the early days of their counseling, Jolene had learned how *de*structive, rather than *con*structive, their inter-actions had been. So she had begun practicing the simple, but sometimes excruciating, act of quietly thinking for ten seconds before responding.

This evening her practice reaped great dividends. Rather than impulsively blurting out hurtful accusations or condemning questions when they got to the parking lot, she remained quiet. Tom, being extra cautious not to justify his behavior or excuse any of his sinfulness in the slightest, chose to remain silent also.

It was a small victory to celebrate as she climbed into her car to drive the rest of the way home. She still had plenty to mull over, and no clear answers yet to the questions racing through her mind. But she was able to thank the Lord for His great grace that had kept her from making the situation worse by lashing out with judgment.

That night, as Jolene spent time journaling about her day she gradually came to a conclusion.

She was at another crossroad in their relationship; this time she was being challenged to trust even though her rational mind screamed out in protest.

Human reasoning reminded her of all Tom's transgressions; he had totally betrayed her trust during their marriage, emo-tionally as well as physically. Often his self-preservation had caused him to act deceitfully or even outright lie to her. How could she be sure what she had experienced today wasn't just more of the same?

As she mulled these thoughts over something became obvious to her. In spite of having worked through forgiveness, she still had a long ways to go in order to learn to trust again. In her mind she knew those two attitudes, or acts of the will, were not even necessarily connected. In fact, it was entirely possible to forgive someone without reconciling or ever trusting them again.

Yet a deeper question quietly coursed through the confusion in her spirit and settled in her heart. *Who* was she really being called to trust right now; *Tom* or *God*?

One was totally trustworthy, the other was obviously a weak and fallible human who had hurt her time and time again, and could very easily do so again in the future.

A Biblical principle she had recently read suddenly flashed through her mind: the awesome act of learning to walk in faith often begins by placing trust in God, even when we don't understand.

She recalled the falling stars on the first night of counseling and the assurance her Father had spoken to her heart, "You can trust Me!"

So...would she trust *God*, even if she couldn't trust *Tom*?

Because of all she had been through and the faithfulness with which God had carried her each step of the way, her answer to that question was a fairly simple and resounding, "Yes!"

But The Spirit's work in her for the moment was unrelenting. She sensed Him digging deeper, asking an even more probing question. If she could trust God, could she trust that He was working and living *in* Tom?

Jolene was convicted to the core by a new insight this question forced her to consider.

In reality, her current struggle actually said more about lack of trust in *God* than in her ex-husband. By doubting Tom's trustworthiness she was actually making a statement about what she believed *God* capable—or *in*capable—of doing.

Recalling a verse her spiritual mentor had once shared with her, Jolene paraphrased Proverbs 21:1, personalizing it by adding Tom's name: "The changing of [Tom's] heart, as the changing of a course of a river, is in the hand of the LORD." In other words, Tom didn't have to change himself. The Lord would do the changing work. And without a doubt *God* could be trusted!

With that thought, she made a fresh commitment to view Tom as a new creation in Christ, innocent until proven guilty, from this day forward, knowing full well that in order to do so, she would simply have to trust God's almighty power working *in* and *through* him.

By placing her confidence in an Almighty God, instead of man, she had confidence she would not be disappointed.

Eventually the two of them agreed to meet at McDonalds in El Paso, IL, often going through the drive through together before carpooling from there to the appointments. Jolene was impressed and touched by Tom's gentlemanly behavior as he paid for her food each time, appreciating the small, but gracious, gesture and the way it made her feel.

During the hour-long drive to their appointment, they initially kept their conversations very superficial. Primarily focusing on the food they were eating or the weather outside, they were careful to save anything personal or possibly controversial for the safety of Ron's presence.

Both Tom and Jolene appreciated the opportunity to share what they had been through and learn to deal with trust and family issues in a professional setting. During the meetings, Ron sometimes took on the role of provoker, in a sense, asking probing questions that shot to the heart of the matter. In spite of that, Jolene felt safe and secure addressing difficult issues, always confident Ron would assist in diffusing the tension if it became too much for them to handle.

Each month she found herself arriving full of questions and at the same time hungry to learn from the mistakes of the past.

It didn't escape either Tom or Ron's notice that being willing to spend six hours round trip once a month to attend a one or two hour meeting was a substantial sacrifice for Jolene to be making. They were both confident it had to be motivated by more than mere curiosity. Still, they were careful not to put any pressure on her, choosing to accept it for the time being with no questions asked.

In the meantime, Ron wisely counseled Tom to make serving the Lord his top priority, reminding him living a fully surrendered life would achieve much more in the way of softening Jolene's heart than any meager human effort could ever accomplish.

So Tom focused on living a life sold out to Jesus...all the while he continued praying for a miracle.

Chapter 15

*G*radually, Jolene's heart began to soften further.

Several times her Bible fell open to the intriguing book of Hosea. Reading carefully she discovered parallels to her own situation and prayed for insight to clearly understand any principles God was revealing to her through this book written thousands of years earlier.

The story of Hosea had always been puzzling. Because marriage represents God's holy and sacred commitment to His people, it seemed almost ludicrous that The Lord would desire one of His very own prophets to choose a wife whom He knew would be unfaithful.

Yet that is exactly what He had done by commanding Hosea to marry Gomer.

Just as God had forewarned, it wasn't long before Gomer deserted her husband for a life of adultery. In spite of the betrayal, Hosea continued treading the difficult path of obedience, following God's instruction to seek out and rescue her from the life she was living. At his own personal expense he paid to redeem Gomer, buying her back as his wife once more.

Jolene understood God had allowed, and even ordained, these unusual circumstances to serve as an object lesson to His own people. At the time, the children of Israel were committing spiritual adultery by joining themselves to other nations and idols. Hosea's pursuit of Gomer in spite of her infidelity served as a poignant portrayal of God's redeeming love and mercy for His people. The point was crystal clear. Like Gomer, God was ready and willing to forgive and welcome His people back upon their return to Him.

Although it may have primarily been an historical lesson for the Israelites, this story hit home to Jolene.

Especially as she read the notes on 1:2-3 in her Life Application Bible:

"It is difficult to imagine Hosea's feelings when God told him to marry a woman who would be unfaithful to him. He may not have wanted to do it, but he obeyed. God often required extraordinary obedience from His prophets who were facing extraordinary times. God may ask you to do something difficult and extraordinary, too. If He does, how will you respond? Will you obey Him, trusting that He who knows everything has a special purpose for His request?"

Hosea had been instructed to give Gomer another chance without any assurance from God she would remain faithful this time.

Jolene wondered if perhaps God was asking the same of her.

A fledgling seed of faith began to sprout in her heart as she considered the idea. Perhaps God could still bless their relationship and use it for His glory, in spite of Tom's past unfaithfulness. And even if there was no guarantee that the future would be free from hurt and pain.

Frankly, the thought frightened her beyond belief. She definitely wasn't ready to make any commitment yet, but at least she was beginning to entertain the possibility of moving towards reconciliation at some point in the future, IF that was where God led.

Around this time Jolene began talking with a good friend and mentor who had gone through a similar experience in her own marriage. This dear woman had also walked through the pain of adultery followed by divorce before eventually remarrying the one who had betrayed her. Having a friend who could truly empathize with every step of the journey was a huge encouragement to Jolene. Granted, there were times when observing this friend walk through the healing process a few steps ahead of her scared Jolene immeasurably. But the wisdom that stemmed from personal experience was invaluable and helped Jolene immensely whenever doubts and fears arose in her own journey. Witnessing firsthand the faithfulness of God in restoring her mentor friend's marriage after adultery and divorce became one of Jolene's biggest sources of hope. If Jesus did it for them, perhaps He would choose to work a similar miracle for her and Tom!

Sensing more receptivity in Jolene, Ron's gentle encouragement was to begin spending more time together outside his office, talking openly and honestly with one another, and each getting to know the other one better than ever before. At this point they recognized this was nothing at all like two teenagers simply playing around with a relationship, or a couple dating without a purpose; they were entering into something much more serious. Their whole intent was to consider marriage. In light of that, Ron labeled this stage in their relationship "courting"; a term Tom originally laughed at as stuffy and old-fashioned, before realizing Ron was serious.

Shortly after they had made a commitment to give courting a try, Tom drove up to attend the girls' school conferences along with Jolene. Afterwards the two of them headed to Starbucks and talked together awhile.

While sipping their coffee, Jolene asked Tom about his work goals, finances, and ideas regarding the future.

Among other things, Tom assured her IF they were to seriously consider reconciliation down the road, he would definitely be open to the idea of moving to Elgin so she and the girls wouldn't be uprooted.

The selflessness in this comment warmed Jolene's heart and encouraged her that God truly must be at work in Tom's life. It definitely hadn't escaped her notice how he had purposefully prefaced the sentence with "If". She appreciated the fact he wasn't being presumptuous or pushy.

But it was his openness to the idea of living in Elgin which absolutely stunned her.

During their years apart, she had come to understand just how much they had allowed the conflict in marriage to center on their individual backgrounds and families. Instead of meshing the way they'd each been raised and blending it into their own unique, God-honoring family style, they had both held stubbornly to their own upbringing as the only "right" way to do things.

Of course this attitude made for many arguments. Oftentimes in her frustration Jolene had finally resorted to hashing out issues with her parents. By doing so she could usually rely on someone to sympathize with her perspective. Due to that fact, there had been considerable tension between Tom and his in-laws, to the point he had grown to resent any time she spent with her family.

So being agreeable to live near them was, to Jolene, further tangible evidence of God at work in his heart.

Nestled in a corner of the quiet café that afternoon, Jolene found herself letting her defenses down more than usual around Tom. Because of the consideration he had shown, she felt safe enough to share her own thoughts regarding the possibility of remarriage.

Candidly speaking from the heart, she assured him she was finally willing to acknowledge the possibility God might draw them back together down the road. But if He did, she wasn't willing to accept anything less than a God-honoring marriage the second time around. Therefore she wasn't ready to move forward until she was completely confident they were in total agreement and would both invest all their energy into building a marriage that would bring glory to the Father.

With total transparency she pressed on, verbalizing the questions and fears that sometimes kept her awake at night:

Would she learn to love him again?

What if she were to remarry, only to be betrayed a second time?

Could her heart endure the humiliation and pain of another affair?

Yet, as excruciating as a failed marriage or second affair would be, one of her biggest fears at this point was the thought of ending up in a mediocre marriage, with no Biblical justification to leave. As she bluntly stated, "I'd prefer being single the rest of my life rather than having a second marriage fail. But

187

worse yet would be the misery of being stuck in a stifling, dead marriage with no escape!"

Tom listened attentively to her words and simply nodded in agreement. No anger, no justification, no finger-pointing.

Jolene had no doubt now. God definitely *had* gotten a hold of Tom's heart!

As she comforted herself with that thought, she forged ahead, sharing an idea that had just come to mind recently. Posing it as a question, she asked Tom his thoughts on each of them beginning to put money aside every month so that, if things worked out in the future, they would have a stash of money to use for a trip together. She promptly put out a disclaimer that if things didn't work out they would both have money saved to be used elsewhere.

She was thankful when he supported the idea, although as soon as he suggested opening one account with both their names on it, she suddenly wanted to backpedal and retract the whole idea. His argument that a joint account would symbolize a commitment to each other seemed valid enough, to be sure. But she still wondered if they were getting ahead of themselves and would be better off keeping the money separate, combining it later if appropriate. In spite of her reservation she decided to go along with his idea for now, agreeing to a mutual account into which they would each make direct deposits on a regular basis.

But at the same time she made a mental note to run the plan past Ron to get his opinion on the matter.

Eventually, the mood lightened somewhat as they brought each other up to speed on their lifestyle, likes, dislikes, and opinions on a wide range of subjects. As they talked, both Tom and Jolene were in awe to find their viewpoints aligned more closely than they ever had during marriage. In fact, although the past five years had brought considerable change to both of their lives, God had somehow brought them to the same place at the same time in multiple ways.

Tom's relationship with Jesus was vastly different now than it had been when his focus had been primarily on man's approval, rules and religion rather than Christ. Admitting to his fear that Jolene might not be ready to accept his life with the Lord for what it was, he was delighted to learn just how much her relationship with Jesus had also blossomed and how similarly they now viewed the Christian walk.

Writing in her journal that night, Jolene was grateful and relieved to be able to record that their first official "outing" had gone well.

Building on the positive experience, a week later Tom drove back up for Shayna's kindergarten program at school. After years of missing their dad's presence at activities, Shelby and Shania were beaming at the chance to sit in the audience between both of their parents. Shayna, too, looked extra pleased as she came out on stage, delighted by the simple knowledge her mommy and daddy were sitting together in the audience somewhere.

Witnessing the joy on all the girls' faces brought tears to Tom's eyes and a lump to Jolene's throat.

Once again that evening, Jolene's journal entry simply stated, "It went ok."

With the holiday season approaching and based on the positive interactions they'd been having, Tom decided to invite Jolene to attend his work Christmas party. So he was somewhat disappointed when she responded that it was much too soon to attend that type of social event together.

Sometimes it seemed to him that for each step forward, she withdrew two steps backwards.

Yet, frustrating as it was Tom knew he couldn't hold it against Jolene. Instead, he chided himself for the exasperating roller coaster ride he had put her through during their marriage and separation. How many times had he cried to her, begging to work things out, only to yell a day or two later that it was all over and he was through trying?

So, although it wasn't easy, he knew he must be patient and allow God to direct the timing and course of their relationship. In the meantime he would keep chasing hard after Jesus, delighting in the knowledge that Jolene, too, was running the same direction.

He envisioned the day they would join hands and run together like they never had run before. What a day that would be!

For those who are not yet married, or even for those who are, never doubt God's ability to prepare the heart of the one He has planned for you to match the work He is doing in your own heart. All you are asked to do is leave it in His Almighty hands. So many individuals today are desperately seeking a "soul mate" on their own. Rather than pursuing a relationship with another human, God asks you to pour your energy and heart into your relationship with Him, while trusting HE will bring the right human relationship to you in His perfect timing. If you run hard towards Jesus, eventually you may glance to the side and find someone running hard right alongside you. For now, trust Him and His timing as He works to perfectly prepare both of your hearts to be ready at the same moment.

Chapter 16

When Tom's birthday rolled around in November 2007, they decided to celebrate together as a family by taking the girls to Dick's Climbing Wall and then to Buffalo Wild Wings for dinner. Shayna had no recollection of ever going on a family outing with both parents, while Shania had only a few. Even Shelby's memories of being a family unit were fuzzy by now.

As a matter of fact, other than the recent school recital when Tom and Jolene had both been in attendance, and church every now and then, about the only time the girls remembered their parents being in the same place at the same time was every other weekend in Morris at Culvers, their traditional meeting spot for swapping custody. Often thick with tension, those meetings had been far from celebratory!

So this day was extra special, indeed. Not only were they getting to celebrate all together, their dad had driven to their house so the five of them would actually be riding somewhere in one vehicle!

In light of the rare circumstances, all three girls were literally bouncing with excitement as they bundled up and headed, happily chattering, to the car.

Tom and Jolene were careful to keep the conversation lighthearted in their daughters' presence. There was plenty of laughter as they all enjoyed one another's company. So much, in fact, that at one point Shania innocently pointed out that Mommy wasn't frowning as much as she usually did around Daddy. Without hesitation, her sisters emphatically agreed with the observation. Somewhat mortified, Jolene once again realized the girls were much more perceptive than they were given credit for.

When Tom left to head back home, Jolene could sense his appreciation for the afternoon and evening. She was truly thankful he had enjoyed it and that their first family outing had been a success overall. There was no denying it had felt good to be an "intact" family once again, even if only for a few hours.

However, that evening Jolene wrote in her journal, *"I still don't feel anything towards Tom. I'm in a trial period, just testing the waters and not ready to commit to anything yet."*

As she placed the cap on her pen, she re-read what she had just written. The first sentence stood out and made her pause.

Thinking back, she remembered all too well the day she had first admitted to herself that her feelings of love for Tom had virtually disappeared. And the ensuing storm her confession had unleashed.

In spite of all the struggles and conflict they'd faced in marriage, it hadn't been until after living on her own for awhile, functioning fairly well as a single mom, that Jolene had acknowledged she no longer had any of the loving feelings a woman should have towards the man she'd married. It had been such a gradual process she wasn't even sure when the final flames had been snuffed out.

Feeling guilty and ashamed at first, Jolene had kept her lack of feelings to herself for awhile. Eventually, the truth had come out in a conversation with Tom, without her really meaning for it to do so.

It had been sometime during the mandatory two year waiting period for their divorce when Tom had insisted on her meeting him at Culver's to discuss some things.

His outward appearance that evening had not escaped Jolene's notice. The instant she'd walked in the door and caught a glimpse of him sitting in a corner booth, clean-shaven and respectfully dressed, she'd known what she would be hearing from him that evening. Without a doubt he was going to try telling her he was "changing".

Again.

By now Tom's sporadic attempts to "change" had become rather predictable. As had the outcome. It always began with an outward effort on his part to change some of the petty things they had often argued about, like his goatee, length of hair, and choice of clothing. The first few times, hungry for news like this, she had allowed herself to believe the transformation was more than skin deep. Unfortunately it rarely took very long to realize just how shallow he still was, inwardly. No matter how much he changed his outer facade, it was still the same Tom underneath.

So truth be told, over time she had become fairly cynical with very little confidence in his attempts to change. Each time her heart had grown more reluctant to the idea of reconciling with someone who had proven to be so untrustworthy over and over.

When Tom saw her walk in on that particular night, he had nervously risen to meet her at the front counter, where they both placed their usual order. Returning to the booth with trays in hand, they sat down and began sipping their drinks in awkward silence.

Finally Jolene raised her eyebrow questioningly. "Well?" she inquired.

After hedging around for awhile Tom had finally blurted out simply, "Jolene, I'm sorry for what I did, for what I said and how I treated you." Fidgeting with the crinkled paper wrapper from his straw he rushed on, "I don't expect you to forgive me, because

I don't know how I could forgive you if *you* had done these things to *me*, but..."

With that his voice faded away self-consciously, while Jolene waited expectantly, in case there was more. Finally, he finished. "Will you please forgive me?"

With her thoughts in a jumble, Jolene drew an extra long sip to buy herself some time while formulating a response. She desired to forgive him. At least she thought she did. Regardless, she knew she *should* forgive him. But as she sat there twisting a napkin in her lap, she was struck by the hollowness she felt inside. She couldn't deny she was deeply disappointed by what felt like a very superficial apology from him, taking into consideration the depth of the sin, shame and pain inflicted.

Struggling to be somewhat tactful, she decided to let him know exactly how she felt.

"Tom, I'm not trying to pick your apology apart, but sin is very serious and very specific," she began. "It's not that I want to hear all the garbage all over again. But for your sake, it seems you would benefit from recognizing and confessing specifically what you did so that Satan wouldn't have any cracks later through which he can get a foothold in your life."

Although he listened quietly, he didn't offer anything more sincere in terms of regret or confession; just nodded with pursed lips.

If she'd seen below the surface she would have known he was inwardly fuming, as he asked himself why he was surprised by her reaction. It had always been like this. No matter what he did he had always felt it wasn't good enough for Jolene. Now she was even picking apart his apology, for Pete's sake! But he'd kept all of these thoughts to himself.

So, in spite of how Jolene felt about his vague and sweeping apology, she quietly offered to forgive him. Yet she found herself wondering how she would ever truly be able to forgive in the way Christ called her to.

Silence descended upon them as she pondered how to finish saying what was on her heart, knowing it would surely wound him but at the same time sensing it needed to be spoken.

Finally, her lack of feelings had tumbled out in one honest but hurtful rush.

"Tom, the truth is I don't miss you anymore. I really believe I have lost the loving feelings for you that a wife should have for her husband. I've moved on and am actually functioning just fine without you. Unfortunately, I don't see the changes you keep telling me about; there are still too many bad habits that you are hanging on to for me and the girls to get involved with you right now. I'm sorry, but I still need my space for awhile, until you can figure things out and really change from the inside out."

She went on to assure him that this definitely didn't mean she was giving up forever or desiring divorce. She still hoped they could someday salvage their marriage but she desperately needed him to understand there would have to be major change before she could or would consider reconciliation.

It was obvious Tom had been emotionally unprepared for her candor. Conversation between them had been very uncomfortable and brief from that point on. To her surprise, Tom had reacted without any outward anger whatsoever, but his countenance revealed a sense of rejection deeper than any she'd ever seen him struggle with up to this point.

Soon they'd cleaned off the table and headed to the parking lot. By the time Tom reached his truck, tears were silently coursing down his cheeks. As he pulled away crying Jolene sat in her van and began to pray. She had been alarmed to witness just how much of a blow her words had proven to be, and as she'd watched Tom dejectedly pull out of the parking lot, she had felt moved to specifically ask God for His hand of protection from despair or any self-inflicted harm that night.

The next few days Tom had repeatedly contacted Jolene in an attempt to discuss the matter further but she hadn't felt there was much left to discuss at this point. The harsh reality was that her life was simpler in so many ways since they had separated. In fact, it was a relief to be free of the drama, upheaval, and hurt she had dealt with on a daily basis during marriage. And like she'd said, the feelings of love she had once felt for him were simply no longer there. It was glaringly obvious he had a long ways to go to prove he was a new man.

What more could she say?

Yet he had persistently hounded her that week. One evening he called and talked briefly to the girls, then asked Shelby to put her mom on the phone. As soon as Jolene answered he again expressed his concerns; she didn't love him, didn't seem to be praying for her love to grow, nor was she willing to work at getting back together. In fact, he informed her that since she had lost her love for him, he no longer wanted to talk to her, see her, or have anything to do with her whatsoever until her love had returned.

Jolene had been dumbfounded by such a childish and ridiculous manner of attempting to solve the issue.

The conversation had gone on and on in seemingly endless circles. Somehow, Tom seemed to find it perfectly reasonable that he should expect Jolene's unconditional love in spite of the fact he had so often demonstrated a lack of the same towards her.

By the time she hung up she was emotionally exhausted and overwhelmed with frustration at his complete lack of consideration for her feelings, emotions, or convictions. The whole phone call had focused on his wants and desires and only reiterated in her mind why she needed some space for awhile, to help her sort out her own emotions. She had tried to make clear to him one more time this was not the death of their marriage. He just needed to prove himself to her; she needed to see ongoing fruit in his life demonstrating repentance for the mistakes of the past that had led to their current situation. She had also assured him that she was trusting God to give her the desire and love for him again when the time was right.

It seemed to fall on deaf ears.

The next weekend when it came time to swap the girls, it had been Tom's dad who showed up to meet her in Morris, something Jolene had half-expected. However, it soon became apparent Tom had convinced his dad to act as messenger in addition to taxi driver. Handing her a CD, Tom's father had simply said "Someone" thought she should listen to this particular recording of a recent sermon.

Fully suspecting that "Someone" was Tom, Jolene prayed for the right attitude as she began listening on the drive home. It came as no surprise whatsoever to discover the sermon was mainly centered on love, forgiveness, and compassion.

A chuckle escaped her lips at the irony of it all. Tom, who had left *her* and then filed for divorce was now attempting to send her packing on a guilt trip just because she'd had the audacity to admit having lost her feelings for him somewhere along the way. Apparently, her lack of love had suddenly fueled his determination to get her back.

However, in spite of all the emotional dialogue, it hadn't taken long for Tom to give up the most recent pursuit of Jolene and return to his selfish lifestyle once again. In fact, not even two weeks after that conversation in Culver's, Jolene had received reports of a new girlfriend in his life.

The whole thing had proven to be just one more emotional whiplash for her. Although Tom had been extremely concerned by her lack of love for him, it seemed pretty obvious he wasn't all that deeply in love with her anymore. If he were he wouldn't already be involved with another woman, would he?

At the time she'd been so weary of the unending seesaw of emotions. In just a little over a year's time he had taken her on a wild ride, vacillating between pursuing an adulterous affair, asking for her forgiveness, and raising her hopes telling her they would sell the house and start over. Instead he had left her and the girls, refusing all the while to listen to any reasoning about reconciling. When he'd filed for divorce, she'd given him plenty of opportunities to change his mind, all to no avail.

Until shortly after the judge denied his request.

Since then he'd had second thoughts more frequently, but never long term. Then suddenly he seemed to think he had the right to reprimand *her* for not loving *him*! To top it all off, he'd suddenly jumped off the hypothetical teeter totter, causing her to slam down to the ground with a harsh jolt as he dashed away in pursuit of someone new.

At that point all Jolene had wanted to do was dust herself off and climb down from the teeter totter once and for all.

Eventually she had opened up to her spiritual mentor about her lack of feelings and Tom's reaction. In his wisdom he had pointed out to her that love is not primarily a feeling, but rather, Biblical love is a call to action.

It is a *choice* not an *emotion.*

He had gone on to remind her that feelings of affection often follow in the footsteps of loving action and that, because it is a choice rather than a feeling, love *can* be learned again.

There was great comfort in that thought. What she heard him saying was just because her feelings were gone for the time being didn't mean she would never be capable of loving Tom again.

In fact, the more she'd processed it in the months to follow, the more she'd wondered if her lost desire for Tom had really been a simple attempt to end the seesaw ride and protect her own heart from the devastating ups and downs.

Truth be told, in the weeks directly following his affair she had intentionally and deliberately chosen to love him through her actions. But she had grown weary and worn with all the effort of putting Tom above her family, attempting to encourage him in the ways he desired, and pouring every ounce of her strength into doing what she could to save their marriage when all she received in return was further disappointment, discouragement and rejection.

She'd finally determined the more emotionally involved she allowed herself to become the worse off she felt. So with time she had erected walls around her heart in an effort to keep the pain out.

Now almost five years had passed since that awkward conversation with Tom explaining that her feelings for him were pretty much nonexistent. She had to admit she was a smidgen surprised that not even spending an enjoyable day together had stirred any inward feelings for him.

Suddenly a thought occurred to her.

Perhaps she was trying to "feel" in love rather than to "act" in love. But if love was a choice, did it even matter how she felt?

If she could begin tearing down the walls around her heart, brick by brick, maybe love would once again flow freely. Could the key to tearing down those walls be as simple as making a daily choice to demonstrate love, even when she felt none?

In Titus 2, older women in the church are exhorted to teach the younger women how to love their husbands (Titus 2:4). If love were strictly a feeling, that chapter would in effect be instructing women who are more mature to teach others how to feel.

Stop and consider for a moment. Is that even possible?

Perhaps it is possible to impart knowledge as to what type of reaction or emotion is appropriate, but can we truly foster those feelings within someone? Only God can do such a thing as we yield our entire mind and spirit to Him. Rather, God was charging Titus 2 women with the responsibility of demonstrating how to live out love towards their husbands and children in very real, practical ways. Feelings may ebb and flow but true love is able to remain constant throughout the tides of life because it is simply a daily decision being put into practice.

Throughout the ages, 1 Corinthians 13 has fondly been called "The Love Chapter". Therein we can find God's definition of true agape love:

"Love is patient, love is kind and is not jealous; love does not brag and is not arrogant, does not act unbecomingly; it does not seek its own, is not provoked, does not take into account a wrong suffered, does not rejoice in unrighteousness, but rejoices with the truth, bears all things, believes all things, hopes all things, endures all things. Love never fails..." (1 Cor. 13:4–8 NASB)

Looking through that list, nowhere will we find love described as a warm fuzzy emotion or feeling towards another person. Instead, what we read are various decisions and actions we are called to make in order to foster true love.

What our culture calls "love" is often mere infatuation or simple lust. Again, neither of those comes anywhere close to God's definition of love.

In the world's definition, love is selfishly centered on how the other person makes us feel. God calls us to a higher standard; we are called to emulate the selfless agape love Christ modeled for us.

As He hung on the cross He wasn't considering how He felt towards us and if we were worthy of the price He was paying. Instead His focus was simply on fulfilling what His Father had required of Him.

In other words, His love was a decision; an act of obedience!

In reality, it may have been our sin which sent Him to the cross, but it was love that held Him there that day.

Chapter 17

For quite awhile Tom had been calling Jolene every Tuesday night at 8:30 p.m. Demonstrating she was a priority in his life was an important step for him to take in repairing some of the damage done to their relationship. Ron assured him consistency was much more important than the content of their calls.

These weekly conversations, as well as the time spent driving back and forth from counseling sessions, provided ample opportunities to practice better communication skills. They had been given four principles to work on and were grateful to have some clear-cut guidelines to direct them:

Principle #1: Be honest

Obviously, there had been plenty of deceit in their relationship throughout Tom's affair and cover-up. But the lack of honesty ran deeper than merely *spoken* lies.

Sometimes the dishonesty hadn't been in the form of what *was* said but, more so, what *wasn't.*

Although Jolene was by nature more outspoken, when it came to her own feelings and emotional needs there had been plenty of times she hadn't openly expressed her expectations to Tom. In her mind, it had seemed if he loved her enough it should be unnecessary to verbalize her needs; he should just instinctively know what they were.

In turn, each time he'd failed to meet her unspoken expectations she'd grown frustrated and hurt. Sometimes sensing her disappointment, Tom would find himself baffled as to what on earth he'd done wrong *this* time. Not wanting to dig himself deeper into whatever hole he'd obviously just tripped into, he'd typically dealt with her displeasure by withdrawing. This, of course, only served to further aggravate her.

The problem went both ways. Tom, too, had been wounded by his own unvoiced, unmet needs on multiple occasions. Rather than holding himself responsible for failing to voice his expectations to Jolene, he'd grown resentful towards her for failing to love him the way he desired; the way he had observed his mom love his dad.

Now, as Jolene delved deeper into the art of communication and, more specifically, love languages, it finally dawned on her why there had been times she'd had the strange sense she and Tom were speaking entirely different languages.

In reality they had been!

Although Tom hungered to be built up with words of affirmation in order to understand how much she loved him, Jolene had felt it completely unnecessary to repeatedly verbalize her appreciation to him. Not intentionally withholding what he longed to hear, she had just assumed that having said something one time was sufficient. She figured once she had spoken it he knew where she stood and could count on her feelings remaining the same unless she told him differently.

If only she'd known how far a few simple words would have gone towards refilling his rapidly depleting love tank.

It had bothered Jolene immensely whenever Tom had run home to his mom. She simply hadn't understood the reason why. The fact was Tom's mother spoke his love language well, affirming and expressing her affection through spoken words, actions and motherly concern. Therefore he had expected nothing less from his own wife. But to Jolene's practical nature, treating him in the way he was accustomed to would have felt as if she were babying an adult. Because it didn't come naturally to her she rarely went out of her way to fuss over Tom, shower him with appreciation, or make him feel like the center of the world.

Now, as they discussed their needs in terms of their growing understanding of the languages of love, Tom related a simple example that Jolene found laughable...until she realized just how serious he was.

Shortly after they had returned from their honeymoon they had made their first trip to visit her parents. Fighting homesickness, Jolene had been so grateful for the opportunity to see her family that she had expressed her gratitude and thanksgiving to Tom multiple times as they travelled back home from their weekend in Elgin.

Her appreciation had touched him deeply. Knowing he had made his wife happy actually served to make *him* feel loved.

So the next time he'd agreed to a trip to her parents' he had expected praise and thanksgiving once more. But as far as he could remember she'd never again expressed any appreciation when he'd consented to a visit with her family. She seemed to feel entitled to the visits, which truly bothered him.

In his mind, he'd believed he was being generous each time he'd taken Jolene back to Elgin or allowed her to make the trip on her own. Especially if he permitted himself to dwell on his own Grandma's infrequent visits back East once she moved to the Midwest. Having left her family to marry his grandfather, she'd been perfectly content in her new life with her husband, rather than continually pleading to be taken back "home".

Prior to and during his engagement Tom had imagined a marriage in which love would run so deep he and his wife would be fully satisfied with one another's company. He had entered marriage with unrealistically high expectations of Jolene putting him first at all times.

So when she often desired or, worse yet, actually seemed to *need* spending time with her family he'd felt deprived of her single-minded devotion. In his insecurity he'd wondered why he wasn't sufficient for her and what made her think of her family so often.

To him, the two were exclusive of one another.

The way he saw it, if she wanted to be home with her family, it obviously meant she didn't want to be with him right then. Therefore, the more frequently she'd asked to go, the more resentful he had become of any and all interactions between her and her close-knit family.

Now, as Tom carefully expressed to Jolene how wounded he'd been over those frequent trips, his eyes were opened to clearly discern just how childish his selfish attitude had been. He was ashamed, as he saw it in a new light and realized her desire to spend time with her parents and siblings had been completely reasonable.

More than that, he was beginning to understand it had been her way of giving and receiving love from her relatives. Growing up in a large family, with most of her relatives living near-by, Jolene had been accustomed to celebrating every birthday and holiday with cousins, aunts and uncles, in addition to many other family get-togethers on a regular basis. To suddenly be ripped away from all that and then have to fight him for each and every opportunity to visit had placed an unnecessary strain on their relationship.

It was a strain which candid communication on both their parts may have helped to alleviate.

Truly, neither of them had intentionally set out to deny the other one's needs. The problem really had been ignorance. Both had been oblivious to how desperately the other had needed them to speak in their own language of love.

Just as Tom's longing had been for words of affirmation and appreciation from her, it was obvious now that Jolene had craved quality time, not only with her family, but also with Tom.

In fact, some of her most contented moments during marriage had been the days spent working side by side with him on various projects around the house and yard. Always willing to work hard, she had enjoyed the intimacy of laboring together and creating something through their combined efforts.

She'd never understood why she had felt so disconnected from Tom as the little girls had been born and taken more and more of her time. Instead of carving out moments for each other they had "divided and conquered"; as Jolene had poured more of her energy into the household work, Tom took on more of the outdoor tasks.

Once he began the nighttime shift, the quantity and quality of their time together had been depleted even further. With him working during the night and sleeping a good share of the morning, there had been very few moments left for connecting with one another.

Since neither of them seemed to know what kind of deposit to make into the other's "love account", they had both unwittingly drained the balance dry.

The pain they'd caused one another had rarely been deliberate in nature, but they were now fully aware just how a constructive conversation conveying their true needs, feelings, and emotional wounds could have saved years of misery.

As a result, they now chose to focus on the importance of honest communication in every way possible. Avoiding outright lies required little effort on either of their part anymore, as it was a natural component of their current Christ-centered lives. On the other hand, being willing to express their needs carefully and respectfully proved to be a much greater challenge than either had expected it to be. Old habits die hard and they both discovered it required a conscience effort to willingly articulate what they desired in an open and honest manner, rather than unfairly expecting the other to read their mind.

During their five and a half years of living together prior to separating, they had gone to bed angry with one another for a multitude of reasons, too many times to count. Sometimes for days, or even weeks on end, they had allowed issues to simmer below the surface like a volcano. The pressure would build and eventually lead to an eruption, but by then it was no longer just one issue that spewed out. Rather, there would be such a lethal mix of accumulated tension and hurt it often proved to be too overwhelming to deal with in a constructive way.

This was why the second principle was so critical for them to diligently practice.

Principle #2: Keep current

At one point in their marriage Jolene had told Tom their rug was practically four feet tall from all the garbage swept under it.

They'd both known it wasn't healthy to allow problems to fester the way they did but with new issues popping up almost daily they weren't equipped to deal effectively with every conflict that arose. Though Jolene often confronted him immediately, Tom rarely was ready to work out the conflict in her timing and manner, so instead of resolving anything they just continued to lift the corner of the rug and sweep the latest concerns underneath.

Unfortunately, whenever the pile could no longer be contained the whole thing would blow up in their face. At that point, however, they'd find themselves suddenly dealing with multiple issues on so many different levels it was too difficult a mess to unravel. More often than not, when it was all said and done, they'd accomplished very little other than adding to the ever-growing pile under the rug.

In contrast, they now attempted to address any issues that came up as soon as they arose. After all, God must have had a reason to include, "Do not let the sun go down upon your wrath" in His Holy Word. (Eph. 4:26)

Dealing with conflict often proved to be messy. Confronting problems constructively wasn't always peaceful or pleasant. But they learned it was much easier to address one issue at a time rather than several days or weeks' worth at once.

And in the process they discovered why so many of their early attempts at problem-solving had failed.

Principle #3: Attack the problem, not the person

During their marriage, arguments had often escalated into character assassinations rather than focused attempts at fixing whatever the root issue was.

Something as seemingly innocent as Jolene's question regarding the dollar he'd had in his pocket had been known to quickly spiral downward into a yelling match, culminating in personal attacks against one another. In this case, instead of recognizing the issue for what it was—an extremely tight budget that was causing a great deal of stress and tension—Tom had interpreted her inquiry as a lack of trust in him. In reality, Jolene had simply been attempting to track every expense to the penny in order to balance the budget.

But his strong reaction caused her to wonder if, perhaps, he was hiding something from her. As she relentlessly pushed him for more information, she discovered he had, in fact, been deceitful. With finances already stretched to their max, they had needed to lower expenses wherever possible. Viewing soda as a luxury rather than a necessity, Jolene had cut it from the budget. Feeling her decision was an infringement on his rights as the primary provider and head of the home, Tom had continued buying cases of pop and sneaking them into the garage, where he could drink them unseen by her.

Upon exposing his secret stash of soda, suspicion reared its ugly head further and Jolene began to speculate if there were additional items he was buying and hiding from her. At the time, accusations and rapid-fire questions had flown out of her mouth. He'd retaliated with his own share of finger-pointing, eventually storming off to his mom's to bend a sympathetic ear.

In the end, the budget hadn't even been addressed, but both Tom and Jolene went to bed that night feeling completely beaten down by the other.

Without a doubt, effective communication is interwoven and each aspect directly affects the others. In part because of the dishonesty and long-standing conflict, there had typically been plenty of ammunition available for flinging at one another. And fling they had, throwing hurtful accusations like, "You never..." or "Why do you always..." at one another with the precision of an expert archer aiming at his target.

Whoever came up with the adage, "Sticks and stones may break my bones but words can never harm me" was either delusional or lying. The initial pain caused by a hurled stone may be intense, but bruises and breaks usually heal with time. Wounded hearts sometimes never do, especially when the damage is inflicted by one of the most destructive weapons ever wielded: *words.*

What makes spoken words so lethal is that once out of the mouth, they are simply impossible to retract. Lingering in the mind of the listener, they are often replayed, producing fresh pain each time they are repeated.

This was especially true for Tom. With his innate need for affirmation, anything deemed to be less than a compliment in his mind communicated a lack of love for him. Throughout their marriage, countless casual comments made by Jolene had been misconstrued by him to be an assault of his character. As soon as he felt under attack his tendency had been to withdraw or, when he had reached his limit, to strike back and retaliate for all the accumulated wrongs.

Unfortunately, neither tactic was productive in dealing with the real issue at hand.

Under the guidance of their counselor, Tom and Jolene found that practicing the first two principles enabled them to more readily discern the underlying problem as issues arose. As they sought to communicate without tearing one another down, they finally began to make progress on real issues.

It seemed so simple, but it was an epiphany for them as they considered how many times they'd simply focused their energy in the wrong place. No wonder they'd made very little progress in resolving their conflicts. If they had spent the same amount of time and energy attacking the actual problem as they had attacking one another, perhaps their marriage wouldn't have died such a painful death.

At first glance, the fourth principle seemed to be a no-brainer.

Principle #4: Act Christ-like rather than react sinfully

As maturing Christians, Tom and Jolene were well aware they were called to act Christ-like. This meant arming themselves

217

with the full armor of God and displaying the fruit of the Spirit in their lives regularly.

But it went so much deeper than that.

"Act, not react." In reality, Christ-like actions aren't necessarily the difficult part. *Reacting* without sin is.

Tom and Jolene began unpacking this principle by considering how often their conflicts had been initiated, not by an *action*, but a *reaction*. They concluded there had been many times the original action or conversation may have been truly innocent but, when misunderstood or misconstrued by the other one, had brought about a reaction that was far from Christ-like. From that point it was typically a rapid downward spiral from one sinful response to another.

The Bible tells us "...there is no new thing under the sun" (Eccles. 1:9) and also "no temptation has overtaken you except such as is common to man..." (1 Cor.10:13) Based on these and other Scriptures it is clear that every time a person is confronted by a temptation, they can be assured someone else has also faced a similar test, including Christ Himself. Throughout the ages, Satan has yearned to thwart God's plans and purposes in the hearts of His people. His devious strategy has been to place various lures in front of individuals, and then, after careful observation, remember how they react.

Far too few Christians stop to consider what a great disadvantage Satan actually has in this world. Unlike God, he is NOT omniscient (all-knowing). Based on his careful scrutiny of the human race since the Garden of Eden, he seems able to predict the outcome of most situations with a great deal of accuracy, for sure. But because he is incapable of reading the mind, it is strictly guesswork on his part.

While Satan's tactics certainly appear brilliant on the surface, truth be told, he is not very original! As soon as he discovers something that triggers sinful reactions in an individual, he tends to repeatedly use the same bait over and over, expecting (and most of the time reaping) the same results. Only the disguise in which he dresses the bait differs from time to time.

The antidote to his scheme, though incredibly simple in theory, is extremely difficult to implement:

Do not react; at least not outwardly!

Keeping one's reaction hidden from Satan's view causes him to lose his power in the situation and be thrown off his game.

It was encouraging and even liberating for Tom and Jolene to grasp this truth. During marriage, for example, if Jolene had made a comment that Tom perceived as accusatory, he would have been inclined to react either by withdrawing or blowing up. When Jolene would then react by attempting to confront the issue further, often in a tone that conveyed her anger and frustration, what may have began as an innocent comment triggered a crazy cycle. In the end, the only winner was Satan.

219

Instead, by applying principle number four in their current relationship, they learned the best reaction was usually no immediate reaction at all.

This was where Jolene's newfound quietness came into play. Instead of a quick retort that could lead her dangerously close to sinful territory, she now trained herself to silently ponder her answer for at least ten seconds before replying. Usually this was enough time to bring her response into obedience to Christ so that she was *acting* Christ-like rather than *reacting* sinfully.

Tom, too, learned to thwart Satan's schemes. Rather than exploding in anger or retreating to sulk, he attempted to keep any negative reaction to himself. By keeping his thoughts contained, he would cause Satan to lose the upper hand. Instead of withdrawing in a way that shut Jolene out completely, he was beginning to learn how to civilly voice that he needed some space and time to consider what had just happened and even set a future time or date to continue the discussion. This way she knew he wasn't just running away from the conflict but it gave him time to calm down and consider how to respond correctly.

For both of them, it was outright warfare against their nature, but all they'd been through had taught them individually how to depend on Christ for the strength necessary to fight their battles.

As time went on, these four principles didn't require quite as much conscious effort to implement. With practice, they were even becoming the default for each of them. With better communication habits came less tension and conflict. Jolene found herself relaxing and enjoying the interactions with Tom much more.

As winter wore on and Valentine's Day approached Tom found himself in a dilemma.

Throughout their separation and since the divorce, he had often been generous with trinkets and purchases for Shelby, Shania, and Shayna. Now he realized it had been a measly attempt on his part to somehow compensate for the pain his choices had inflicted upon the girls. Back then, his generosity in the way of material "things" had proved to be a source of contention between him and Jolene. She'd clearly seen it for what it was.

Now that he understood where Jolene's irritation and frustration had been coming from he was trying to be more careful in the area of gifts and anything she might view as unnecessary "pampering" or spoiling on his part. Rather than bestowing the girls with fluff to appease his own guilt he now tried to shower them with more precious commodities of time and Biblical leadership on their weekends together.

However, throughout January he had been travelling quite a bit on business, which took him away from them even more than usual. Feeling it could be justified under the circumstances, he had picked up inexpensive gifts to give his daughters upon his return from each trip. This was far different than his old tendency of succumbing to their whining for candy, nail polish or hair accessories purely out of guilt.

Although Jolene had repeatedly informed him she didn't expect anything for herself, on a few occasions he had purchased something small for her anyway. If nothing else, he simply wanted her to know she was on his mind even while they were apart. However, as he thought it over, he became concerned she might view the gifts as a means of pressuring her into a decision about their future. So in one of their weekly phone conversations he asked point blank how she was feeling towards him by now and what her thoughts were regarding the future.

In reply, Jolene shared both good and bad news with Tom.

The good news: she was over her extreme fear of being emotionally hurt by him and no longer felt like running as fast and as far as she could every time he called or came for a visit.

However, the bad news: she was perfectly content with the way things currently were, and as of now had no interest in attempting to move their relationship forward.

He was greatly relieved when she went on to say she desired to continue their joint counseling sessions. Tom was beyond grateful she was willing to maintain the meetings and ended the call by reassuring her once again he would not pressure her to get back together now or ever.

However, after hanging up he found himself second-guessing his response. Should he be pushing harder for reconciliation, since that was what his heart truly longed for? Was he being deceitful by saying he was willing to accept things as they were when deep down he desired so much more? And when it seemed God had begun nudging open the door to that possibility right when Tom had determined to surrender all his hopes?

Instinctively he felt as if he was better off not showing or verbalizing just how much he desired to get back together. Not that he was trying to play mind games with her, but he sensed that if he revealed his hopes and dreams for their future prematurely she would become frightened and completely shut down towards him. For now he was willing to patiently wait and trust God to put the pieces back together in His time and way, if it was His will.

But with Valentine's Day just around the corner Tom was so unsure how to handle it without making her uncomfortable he ended up emailing his counselor for advice. Usually Tom gave each of his daughters a single red rose to celebrate the holiday. Now he found himself in a stew, wondering if he should also get a single rose for Jolene...or perhaps a full bouquet of roses. On the other hand, maybe he should buy her something else entirely? Or would it be best to buy nothing at all?

Ron responded with a simple assurance that to err on the side of showing he cared was most likely the best choice. His recommendation was to go ahead and give her a single rose, similar to the girls'. In his opinion, that would demonstrate he was thinking of her without appearing overly excessive.

Truth be told, as simple as the gesture had been, it had truly touched Jolene's heart. Which completely confused her. It sometimes seemed like her heart and head just weren't in agreement or moving forward at the same pace. In her mind she was convinced she was fine with the status quo, leaving everything how it was. But her heart felt growing compassion and even a stirring of appreciation for the man Tom was obviously becoming.

Could there be room in her heart for him once again?

Chapter 18

Throughout the spring and early summer Tom and Jolene continued to spend time together, most often with the girls present, much to their delight!

Tom made a point of faithfully attending his daughters' school programs, and many Sundays he drove up to attend church with the four of them. On those occasions they usually went out to eat as a family afterwards. For Jolene, the thought of sharing a meal together at her house still seemed too intimate, so she was thankful he was willing to keep to the neutral ground of restaurants for the time being.

The more they were together, the more convinced Jolene became that God truly *had* done an amazing transformation in Tom's life. By now there had been many opportunities for his true colors to be revealed and yet he remained consistently different from the man he had been during their marriage. She noticed he no longer rationalized his behavior away but seemed to humbly own full responsibility for all the mistakes of his past as well as the present. On multiple occasions he had expressed true sorrow for the pain he had caused not only her, but also the girls and even her parents. His attitude was a great consolation to Jolene.

Another noticeable change was his very obvious shift in perspective away from himself. During marriage, one of her major frustrations had been how "Tom-centered" he had often seemed to be. He consistently thought of how *he* felt, what *he* wanted, why *he* was entitled to something, rather than stopping to consider how it made *her* feel, what *she* desired, or why he might need to surrender his "rights" in certain areas.

That attitude had carried over into their separation and divorce, manifesting itself in more ways than she would have ever imagined. What had stunned her the most was the outrageous self-pity that had reared its ugly head from time to time. On more than one occasion he had practically whined to her, counselors, or church leadership, "You have no idea how hard this is for *me!*"

"Oh, really?" she had been tempted to sarcastically throw back at him. Did he have the slightest clue how hard it was for *her* and the girls? Yet it was as if he'd expected everyone to pity *him* for the trial his own choices had brought into his life!

In contrast, now Tom had developed an extremely tender heart for the girls as well as her. He was quick to surrender his own rights whenever he recognized doing so was in their best interests. No longer concerned about how hard life was for *him*, he instead showed remorse for how hard he had made life for *them*.

Several times throughout the summer Tom offered to drive the girls all the way to Elgin in order to save Jolene the trip back and forth to meet him in Morris. It was a selfless act which demonstrated just how much he had changed.

On one particular day in mid-July, their mutual cousin was visiting Jolene and rode along with her when she went to swap the girls. As someone who had known both of them all their lives and witnessed their good and bad times, she was stunned at the change she noticed in Tom. Especially the way he looked at Jolene. Climbing back in the car with Jolene, their cousin admitted to being blown away by what she had just seen. Her comments were eye-opening to Jolene. Hearing what someone else observed between her and Tom made her realize their relationship might just be more serious than she wanted to acknowledge.

Gradually Jolene was able to admit Tom was a living, breathing testimony of the truth found in 2 Corinthians 5:17, "Therefore if anyone is in Christ, he is a new creation; old things have passed away; behold, all things have become new." He truly *had* become a new person, as far as Jolene could tell.

Because of this, more and more often she caught herself imagining a future that included Tom.

Truth be told, Tom wasn't the only one who had changed; Jolene had also been transformed by the painful journey her life had taken. The ever-increasing depth of her spiritual maturity was definitely not lost on Tom. He was grateful every day for the woman she had become along the way and how her faith had obviously blossomed beyond anything he'd ever imagined it would. She had once shared a quote with which her mentor had challenged her; "The harsh blows in life can bruise and weaken you so severely they will knock you down...or they can serve to build up calluses which help you grow stronger and better able to stand firm in God's strength." Jolene had become living proof of the latter. Tom sensed a quiet strength in her that had come from having learned to depend on Jesus above all else. She was not callused in a hard-hearted way; rather her heart seemed to be surrounded by a protective layer of faith that kept her from being easily wounded by the enemy's relentless attacks.

Just as Tom now willingly took responsibility for his own sins, he witnessed the same attitude within Jolene. No longer quick to lash out or criticize him, she seemed to purposely weigh her words and bite back the kind of comments that used to sting so deeply. Interactions between the two of them became more and more comfortable as they learned they could trust one another more than they ever had during marriage. Whenever issues arose, instead of either of them pointing fingers at the other one, they were both quick to glance inward and determine what they could have personally done differently to lead to a better outcome.

As the days marched on, walls of hurt that had built up between them over the years continued to crumble into dust at their feet and amazing things began to happen as a result.

A very simple explanation of the mortar used in masonry provides an interesting parallel to what was happening in Tom and Jolene's lives. In masonry, mortar is generally made of three elements; sand, a binding agent, and water. This mixture is used to bind materials such as stone and brick together, filling in and sealing the gaps between building blocks in order to create a strong wall.

The word mortar actually stems from the Latin word mortarium, which means "to crush". As Tom and Jolene continued to break down the walls around their hearts, they were in effect "crushing" all the bad habits out of their relationship. Rhetorically, the powder that remained was by no means a worthless residue. Rather it was just one of the valuable and much-needed components from which they would build a healthy relationship from this time forward. The regrets and mistakes of their past left them with gritty memories and coarse determination what not to do in

229

the future, similar to the grainy texture of sand in mortar mix. This rough consistency in mortar creates tiny air pockets for the other elements to fill in, thus providing both strength and resiliency to the mixture. Likewise, every lesson they'd learned made room for an improvement in how they dealt with one another.

Adding in the new communication tools and skills they were gaining would prove to be the binding agent that would help hold everything together and enhance the bond between them.

And then there was the third and most critical element: water. In a spiritual sense, the Living Water is the Word of God. They would only have the necessary strength to survive if they relied on the power of His Word every day. Attempting to mix mortar without water would prove to be a crucial error, as would any endeavor to rebuild their relationship without the wisdom of the Word.

Mingling these three essentials together – lessons from the past, tools for the future, and most important of all, God's written instructions – would create the necessary adhesive to cement a strong foundation of relational building blocks; trust, sacrificial love, faith, words of encouragement, quality time, etc.

An intriguing aspect of mortar is that it is purposely designed to be weaker than the bricks or blocks that it cements together and is typically considered to be the sacrificial element in masonry. The reason for this is simple. Over time, environmental conditions change and shift, causing inevitable decay. If the building blocks themselves were to crumble, a completely new wall would have to be constructed; something which could prove costly and very time consuming. In extreme cases when the mortar has not been properly mixed or is not repaired in a timely manner, entire walls actually do begin to shift and erode. Unfortunately, all too often a wall in such dire need of repair isn't even deemed worthy of the undertaking and is instead deserted, condemned, and abandoned.

Consider how similar this is to a marriage in which the foundational elements break apart. Tragically, those involved often give up too quickly because the amount of effort required appears overwhelming. However, if proper care or time is not taken to rebuild as quickly as possible, the end result will be an abandoned, broken family.

On the other hand, if the weakest component is the mortar, as intended, any decay or crumbling tends to happen within the mortar itself. Repairing this damage is generally as simple as mixing and adding more mortar into the crack. If done quickly enough there are no lasting effects. In fact, the end result may even be stronger than the original. Likewise in marriage, when the inevitable cracks happen, the wise couple will quickly mix up fresh "mortar" and seal the fissures before they get out of hand, thus ensuring a strong wall that will stand the tests of time.

The beautiful truth was, in order for Tom and Jolene's relationship to be rebuilt, it first had to be torn down. Then brick by brick they began the careful reconstruction of a stronger foundation, filling in the gaps with the proper ratio of "sand, binder, and water".

During this period of rebuilding, Jolene's family was aware she had been attending counseling with Tom but she had intentionally chosen to share very few details about it with anyone; not even her parents. She desired to rely solely on her Heavenly Father to show her what to think and believe about her and Tom's relationship. She was afraid if she disclosed details to those she loved she may be influenced by their opinions. And, truth be told, after all the heartache and fluctuating emotions her parents had watched her endure over the years, she couldn't be certain they would even be in support of reconciliation with Tom. Like any loving and protective parents it seemed natural they would desire to shield her and their precious granddaughters from what they would likely see as inevitable hurt.

So for eight months she had remained tight-lipped about what God was doing in their relationship. Until she had reached a definite peace about what the future held she preferred keeping it between Tom and herself.

As June rolled around, so did her family's vacation. Since her teenage years, Jolene's family had been traveling to the Ozarks. The annual trip had always been a highlight of the summer. As the family had grown and changed over the years they had kept the tradition alive, continuing to escape for a week of bonding with each other every other summer. Renting several condos on the lake, her parents, siblings, nieces and nephews would spend practically every minute of daylight together, and then stay up chatting or playing games long into the night.

The air was alive with excitement as Jolene and the girls packed their suitcases, loaded the car and headed towards St. Louis, where they picked her sister up at the airport. Then, together, they drove to the Ozark resort where they met up with the rest of the family.

Just like every other year, they played, ate, swam, and relaxed together, enjoying every minute.

Only a day into their vacation Jolene found herself struggling to keep mum about her budding relationship with Tom. So on Sunday morning she called him as soon as she awoke. In a rush to meet up with everyone for an informal morning Bible Study, she wasted no time getting to the point. "Is it ok if I share with my family what's been happening with you? Or, with us, I guess I should say?" Before he could answer she blurted, "Only thing is, I need to know right now!"

Hearing the urgency in her voice, Tom knew she needed a quick answer but he felt a little like he was playing Jenga with glass blocks. If he pulled out the wrong piece, the whole stack was going to tumble down and shatter. Admittedly, he was delighted by her desire to disclose details to her family. But he was more than a little concerned what kind of reaction she might receive. He was fully aware that if her family raised any doubts about where she and Tom were headed, it could set her back immensely. At the same time, to refuse to let her tell would definitely be shooting himself in the foot. At least if he consented to her telling the family he had a fifty-fifty chance of it going well. So he told her to go ahead, although with more than a little apprehension.

Hanging up the phone, Tom went to kneel down by his bed. There he bathed the day in prayer, specifically the conversation about to take place in the Ozarks, as well as what it might mean for their future.

For Jolene, worship time with her family was always special but today she found it hard to concentrate as she dealt with a wide range of emotions. Impatience and anxiousness mingled with fear and even a little excitement as she mentally rehearsed how she might break the news.

As soon as her brother finished with a prayer, Jolene knew she needed to seize the moment before the room grew too noisy and everyone scattered this way and that to spend a relaxing afternoon doing whatever they chose. She cleared her throat loudly to get their attention. Suddenly all eyes, young and old, were on her. Many looked perplexed, wondering why she looked so serious...and why her eyes were suddenly beginning to brim with tears.

What happened next astonished her right along with the others. Not usually an overly emotional person, it seemed that all her pent up feelings unexpectedly made their way to the surface and bubbled over. Sitting there with her surprised family gathered around, Jolene barely managed to choke out, through heaving sobs, "Could we have an adult meeting tonight?"

In one accord they agreed and promptly made plans for the kids to play together in one condo while the adults met in another after supper that evening.

That afternoon, some of the group went for a boat ride together. Sitting between her mom and brother, Jolene was touched by the concern they expressed over her emotional episode earlier that day. Quietly, they asked if she was ok. Jolene assured them she was fine and just wanted to share what God had been doing in her life. She went on to state matter-of-factly, with very little emotion, "I really don't know why I cried earlier!" Seeing her back to her typical, practical self visibly set her family members at ease.

Basking in the sunshine that afternoon, she had plenty of time to think. Although she had come on this vacation with no intentions of revealing details about her relationship with Tom, she fully believed the timing was right and was grateful for the opportunity to finally share with her loved ones the amazing work of God in both Tom and her own life. No matter what the outcome, her deepest desire for the conversation was for Jesus to be lifted up on high. Without a doubt the story she planned to share was of a repentance and redemption so remarkable, only Christ could have authored it, so He alone was worthy of praise.

After a full day Jolene, her girls and only sister ate a simple supper together in their condo. Chatter was lighthearted throughout the meal as they caught up on stories from her sister's mission work in Mexico. Soon they were cleaning off the table and herding the kids next door to play while the adults all came together to visit in privacy.

The meeting couldn't have gone better if she had scripted it.

Her dad, mom, sister, and three brothers along with their wives, listened intently as she shared details about Tom going to counseling, her conversations with Ron on two separate occasions when he visited her church, and how it led up to joint sessions for her and Tom. The falling stars, verses she had read, what God had been revealing to her, how Tom had proven himself over and over, conversations with her mentor, and finally the way her feelings had begun to soften towards him in recent weeks all spilled out of her.

It took a couple hours to express all that was in her heart and she was thankful the kids remained happily occupied in the other condo the entire time so the grown-ups could listen without interruption.

In the end, all nine surrounded her with overwhelming support. Declaring they wouldn't stand in her way if she was able to forgive him, they assured her they would gladly welcome Tom back into the family if the relationship worked out. Before ending the meeting, everyone gathered around and embraced her, one by one. Basking in their love, Jolene was beyond grateful for a family that loved her enough to support her unconditionally. Even more, she realized just how blessed she was to be surrounded by relatives who loved and trusted God enough to desire what *He* desired, even if it didn't make perfect sense to them.

All in all, it had proved to be an awesome evening of praising God for His faithfulness and unparalleled ability to change the hearts of His children.

Following the disclosure to her family, both Tom and Jolene's expectations were admittedly running higher. For the first time they were both ready to acknowledge their relationship seemed to be moving towards the next stage.

The possibility of remarriage at some point down the road was actually beginning to be a reality!

But as many throughout the ages, including great Biblical characters like Moses, Elisha and Jonah have experienced, it isn't unusual for a deep valley to follow directly on the heels of a great victory.

Chapter 19

About a month after the family meeting, something abruptly changed in Jolene's attitude. She had been feeling unsettled for several days but wasn't able to put her finger on the cause.

Besides counseling appointments, most of the time when they went anywhere together they took the girls with them and made it into a family outing. Not once had Tom pushed Jolene for any physical contact, not even so much as holding hands. Up until this point he had treated her with utmost respect and honored her wishes to keep their relationship entirely in the "getting to know one another again" stage.

However, in light of the recent events in the Ozarks, Tom had worked up the courage to ask Jolene out on a "real" date night, without the girls, one Friday night. She had initially accepted the invitation without reservation but now as she sat across the table from him at Olive Garden, waiting for their breadsticks and salad, her vague sense of uneasiness suddenly intensified.

Perhaps it was the terminology, "date night" that made her uneasy. Or simply that it suddenly felt like a little too much, too fast.

Finally Jolene decided to speak her mind.

"Tom, I think we need to slow down," she informed him hesitantly. "I'm just not ready to be remarried."

Her words hung in the air between them. Out of habit, she reached up and rubbed her nose nervously as she waited for him to break the silence. Watching him intently she noticed a slight twinge of the muscle in his temple; a sure sign he was restraining himself from saying what he really wanted to.

In reality, Tom's immediate response had been, "You've got to be kidding me!" But, thankfully, he had the restraint to keep the thought to himself. The old Tom would have most likely exploded and reminded her just how excruciatingly slow he *had* been taking it.

Truly, he was more than a little puzzled, as he wondered how they could go any slower than what they had been! He hadn't so much as touched her hand once. Nor had he pushed her to make any commitments, whatsoever, about their future. In fact, he had reiterated on multiple occasions that he would not push her now, or ever, to get back together.

After all his painstaking attempts of being extremely careful *not* to give even the slightest implication of being pressured, he was completely baffled how it was even remotely possible for her to suddenly think they were moving too fast.

While he was processing all these thoughts, the server carefully set a large salad bowl, basket of breadsticks, and stack of salad plates in front of them. Jolene politely thanked her as she turned to go, but Tom barely even noticed her presence, or the food for that matter. He had suddenly lost his appetite.

Jolene began to carefully dish up the salad before looking across the table at him, waiting expectantly. Coming to his senses, Tom offered to ask a blessing for the food. Even as he audibly prayed with her, he was silently begging God for great grace to demonstrate the power of Christ in response to her unexpected concern.

Finishing the prayer, he carefully placed a napkin in his lap and glanced up.

Choosing his words cautiously, he first questioned Jolene as to what had prompted her sudden fear. When she wasn't really able to give a definite answer he felt his frustration escalating. Struggling to subdue it, he once again reminded himself not to react incorrectly.

Eventually pushing his salad bowl aside, he mulled over the best way to demonstrate he was respecting her concern yet at the same time addressing it in a constructive manner.

"What about tomorrow?" he finally asked.

Originally he had planned to help her and the girls with yard work at her house the next day. Now, after what she had just said, he wasn't sure he'd even be welcome.

Her ambiguous answer failed to clear up his confusion in the slightest. "I've been really tired and would prefer sleeping in tomorrow."

Unsure how to address the issue further or what she desired from him, Tom decided to let it go and changed the subject entirely.

They managed nothing more than surface talk from that point on as they both attempted to ignore the huge elephant that had suddenly pulled up a chair at the table with them. It proved to be an awkward meal as they mainly focused on their food in order to avoid further conversation.

Eventually Jolene checked the time and pushed her chair back. She still needed to get groceries before heading home to the girls. As Tom signaled their waitress for the bill he offered to go with her to the store. His offer sent alarm coursing through Jolene. Getting groceries together seemed far too personal! She just wasn't ready for a step like that so she firmly refused his offer.

Not knowing what he was doing wrong but afraid to take another misstep, Tom shut down and didn't say any more as they walked out to their vehicles.

Leaving the restaurant, they both were frustrated at what felt like old, destructive communication patterns cropping back up at an alarming rate. It definitely hadn't proven to be one of their best nights together and as far as a first date goes had been deeply disappointing!

Rehashing the evening that night before going to bed at a friend's house in the Elgin area, Tom came to a decision. Even if Jolene wanted to sleep in tomorrow, the work still needed to be done and he was quite capable of doing it without her. If he were to show up and do the work himself, perhaps that would demonstrate his willingness to place her needs above his own. He was optimistic that his act of kindness might heal some of the damage done tonight.

Feeling his earlier discouragement lift ever so slightly, he prayed and read the Word, set an alarm and then settled down to sleep.

———∞———

The next morning Tom pulled into her driveway at 6 a.m. Not wanting to wake Jolene, he was glad when Shelby ran out to meet him and then opened the garage door at his request. He began rummaging around looking for the necessary tools to accomplish what he had come to do.

Unfortunately, though he tried his best to be quiet, he obviously failed. Jolene had heard the sound of the garage door and gotten up to see what was going on. Looking out her bedroom shade, she was immediately fuming mad at his unexpected presence. So much for sleeping in like she had hoped! After getting dressed and brewing some coffee she made her way outside, trying to keep her demeanor calm in spite of the anger she felt inside.

Even with her attempt to hide her feelings, Tom's heart sank with his first glance at her face. Innocent and well-meaning as his actions may have been, Jolene had obviously interpreted them entirely differently than he'd intended. To her, it clearly felt as if he were stepping on "her" territory and invading her world without permission.

The morning couldn't have gone much worse. In Jolene's eyes, everything Tom did was incompetent. He ran the chainsaw wrong, piled the brush incorrectly, cut the grass too short, even proved to be too cheerful with the girls.

With every passing minute Jolene's irritation grew. As did Tom's disappointment and misery. In reality, her deepest irritation was with herself. She knew she was blowing it big time and that the way she was treating him was making him feel horrible. A part of her wanted him to feel needed but she knew her reaction was making him feel unwanted instead. Worse yet was having the girls witness her pathetic behavior. She kept telling herself to stop being such a poor example to her daughters...but she just couldn't seem to change her actions or attitude.

Most frustrating of all was that she really didn't even know why she was so mad at Tom or why everything he did was annoying her in such an unrealistic manner today! And why had she seemingly forgotten all the communication and relational tools she'd been learning?

When Tom left that day, defeat was evident in his eyes. It was obvious he had a burning question he was afraid to ask her.

In all honesty, she could guess what he was wondering because she had several questions of her own:

Had all the positive steps they'd taken in their relationship just been destroyed? Were they back to square one? Was there really any hope for a shared future? Or had they just been fooling themselves all along?

Chapter 20

All the details of that day were still fresh in both their minds at their next session with Ron. Within minutes of stepping into the office, Jolene bluntly shared her thoughts to begin the meeting.

"I am NOT marrying Tom. What I told my family last month wasn't true. I'm ready to call it quits."

She went on to communicate her sentiment that everything was moving too fast for her comfort.

Ron quietly listened, then turned to Tom and kindly gave him some advice.

"Tom, right now in this relationship you need to behave yourself like an idling car. When Jolene presses the accelerator, you move ahead. When she puts on the brakes, you obey the cue and stop. Immediately. Remember, none of this is about you or your timing. It's about being ready to move ahead when—and only when—Jolene does. And then you need to keep an even pace with her. Not too fast, not too slow."

As Ron continued, Jolene began to relax. It was evident both men were being very respectful of her desires and purposefully trying to let her determine the speed with which they moved ahead.

Eventually, Jolene became aware she was no longer mad at Tom about the incident on Saturday. In fact, come to think of it, she wondered if she ever really had been mad or if her anger was disguising some other emotion.

She now clearly understood his intent in showing up to help with her yard work hadn't been to invade her space or wield control over her in any way. In fact, the caring act of kindness had really demonstrated the selflessness of his character. He had devoted an entire morning to cleaning up her yard, receiving nothing in return but her disapproval.

Continuing to analyze her reaction with the help of Ron, Jolene finally was able to label the true emotion behind her anger as fear.

Truth be told, when her meeting with her family had gone so well it had suddenly made the possibility of reconciliation much more tangible. With that knowledge she had suddenly been attacked with a growing apprehension concerning the future and what it held.

Some close friends of hers were going through difficult times in their marriage and watching their problems play out before her eyes resurrected memories of similar issues between her and Tom, thereby raising fresh concerns in her mind about the sustainability of a second marriage for the two of them.

She had been assaulted by question after question for several days prior to their date night. Was she really ready to take him back or would she just be opening herself up to more hurt and shame? What about the girls? How would they adjust to having both parents together again under one roof? And would she and Tom ever be able to have a truly healthy marriage or would it just end up as something to be endured? She'd asked herself these same questions countless times in the past but they had begun to plague her with a fresh vengeance so that by the time Tom had showed up at her house Saturday morning all the irrational fears had manifested themselves in the form of anger. Tom had just been the unfortunate victim.

Being able to process and rationalize where the emotion had originated helped immensely to alleviate her concerns and soon Jolene felt an inner peace and calm returning.

Once again, her peace pivoted on one simple question; in whom was she placing her confidence? Whenever she was tempted to place it in Tom, apprehension inevitably reared its ugly head while niggling doubts consumed her. Not because of his behavior, but simply because he was a mere human.

Instead, when (and only when) she looked to Jesus to finish the work He had begun in them both, she could confidently rest in peace, trusting the path ahead to Him. She had to remind herself that God is and always will be big enough. If she were forced to face adultery again, God would be faithful to help her through this time like He had the last.

Jolene's morning routine including flipping the daily calendar by her stove to the next page with anticipation of what Scripture she would find each day. One particular morning her eyes lingered on the words of Psalms 56:3-4. Verse three had brought comfort to her girls on many dark, sleepless nights when fear set in. But today it was the next verse which took on new meaning for her situation, as she read both verses: "Whenever I am afraid, I will trust in You. In God (I will praise His word), in God I have put my trust; I will not fear. What can flesh do unto me?"

Suddenly she recalled the comfort she had found in her daily calendar at their old house during the days leading up to their separation. Over and over the verses had spoken about God's grace being sufficient at a time when that was just what she had needed. Now, it seemed she was consistently being blessed with reminders about the trustworthiness of God. Again, He knew exactly what she needed!

⁕

Although Ron's counsel to allow Jolene to be the one directing the timing and pace of their relationship was fitting in light of their situation, the reality of their healing process had proven to be somewhat different. Instead of consistently moving ahead in a straight line initiated by Jolene's comfort level, their journey had been more like a stretchy rubber band. At any given point one might be ahead of the other, out front and ready to take another step forward. Because the rubber band encircled them both, they had to be careful so as not to stretch it too thin along the way. If it were to "snap" it would inevitably sting them both. Many times they would unexpectedly trade places, and the one who had been lagging behind would suddenly jump out and lead the way. Rarely had they been at the same place or traveling the same speed in their thought process regarding the future. Yet God continued to work in both of them, wooing and drawing them ever closer to Him and, in the process, to one another.

In light of that, Jolene requested some time alone with Ron at the beginning of their August session. It had been ten months since their first joint appointment and just one month ago she had been threatening to stop even trying altogether. However, she trusted Ron's counseling expertise and needed to know if he could give his blessing and full support to their relationship. So this day she came with a similar question on her heart to the one that had prompted that first meeting back in October.

"Are you fully confident Tom's change is sincere?" she once again asked Ron, this time even more hesitantly than the first, since so much more seemed to be at stake now.

Before he had time to answer, she hastily threw out several more questions. Questions that hadn't even been on her radar ten months ago, and revealed just how far she had come in her relationship with Tom.

"Is there anything else we need to counsel about or work on? And where do we take it from here – how soon do we begin talking about marriage?"

While Ron thoughtfully pondered her string of questions she went on to remind him her self-imposed five year waiting period wasn't even half over. So she wondered if it was entirely premature for her to be considering anything beyond friendship at this point. Yet she also admitted God hadn't ever instructed her to prove Tom for a full five years; it had simply been a measuring tool that made sense from her limited human perspective.

It didn't really seem fair to allow her personal fears to stand in the way of their family being reunited. The compulsory waiting period she had placed herself under would mean their oldest daughter would be sixteen years old before Jolene would allow herself to even consider reconciliation as an option. At that point, Shelby might only have two or three years left at home in which to enjoy the benefits of an intact family!

As she verbally processed all of this to Ron he made a simple but profound point that would have deep impact on her immediate future.

"Jolene, even if Tom were to prove himself for five years, and you continued to come for counseling every month, then what? Regardless, there will always be a point where you just have to take a leap of faith."

He was right, of course.

There was no arguing with it. Up until now on the occasions she had told God she trusted Him and was placing the future in His hands, it had always been with a five year waiting period planted firmly between the present and future in her mind.

Now the truth of Ron's words stripped away all pretense and cut through every excuse. A step of faith simply required faith, whether in five minutes or in five years.

Ron had gone on to share his opinion that they had talked through all the old issues and he believed the two of them were communicating fairly well for the most part. In fact, he really didn't even know what else needed to be addressed on an ongoing basis. So he encouraged her to keep doing what she was; spending time with Tom, continuing to work on their communication and using the tools with which they had been equipped to deal with past problems as well as any current conflicts that arose. If they were both walking closely with the Lord and trusting Him, Ron boldly asserted they would know how to handle questions about the future when God's timing arrived.

Jolene left his office that day with a fresh understanding. A time was coming when she would need to draw a line in the sand and say, "Ok, God. I'm taking a leap of faith right here and now."

All she needed was a heart ready to obey when and where her Lord asked her to go.

That evening as she flipped her Bible to the Old Testament, she opened to a portion of Psalms 119, the longest chapter in the Bible and one that was chock full of applicable Truths. Like many other Sunday School students in the world she had memorized verse 105 as a child, "Thy word is a lamp unto my feet and a light unto my path." (KJV) With regards to what Ron had said today, reading that verse this evening was like pouring peaceful confirmation over her spirit.

The truth was, even though she might be fearful and anxious about the future, God promised to light the pathway in front of her just as far as she needed to see, but no further.

Perhaps that was how she needed to view her situation with Tom. From this point forward she could trust God to guide her next step and show her the way, but she needed to accept the fact He might not necessarily reveal as much of His plan as quickly as she desired.

Granted, there had been many ups and downs throughout their engagement, marriage, separation, divorce, and even recently during their courtship. But through it all God had carried and sustained her, always faithfully illuminating the path ahead.

Even if it was just one small step at a time.

Venturing into the dark on a starless night with nothing but a flashlight with which to light our path, we tend to take slow, careful steps; trusting each footfall only as far as we can see. In contrast, how much quicker is our stride during the day when we have clear visibility far into the distance? A very important lesson for a Christian to learn is how to depend on Jesus to illuminate the way in the light as well as the darkness. Unfortunately, when our path ahead appears clear it is much too easy to become self-sufficient, relying on self instead of our need for His guiding hand.

In the dark, we may be oblivious to obstacles just outside the glowing sphere of light; however, by focusing only on the path directly in front of us, we can ensure our safety. Taking our eyes off our path and focusing on the hurdles to the side usually leads to inevitable distraction and, worse yet, a stumble or fall. As we gingerly step along the lighted path, little by little the way will open up in front of us. Unless we have an extra powerful beam of light, it is rare to be able to see much farther than a couple feet ahead. Likewise, God often chooses to keep the path ahead of us veiled; sometimes for our protection, sometimes simply to build our faith and trust in Him.

Faith is what fuels our trust. If the batteries in a flashlight grow weak or die, the flashlight is of no use until we replace the dead batteries. It is the same with faith. If our faith dies out our trust will fail, too. Like batteries, faith has to be properly and firmly placed, completely engaged, and connected to the source in order to be beneficial.

Chapter 21

Suddenly Tom and Jolene began to talk more openly and regularly about the prospect of remarriage. It all happened so fast that before they knew it, they were no longer hypothetically discussing marriage as a speculative proposal for the far off future...they actually had a date set and were making plans to break the news to the girls!

Some days Tom was tempted to pinch himself. Could this really be true? There had been times following his affair when he had desperately wished he would wake up to find it had all been a nightmare; now he sometimes feared he might wake to find the relationship he and Jolene were rebuilding had simply been a magnificent dream.

As each new morning dawned full of promise for the future, Tom rose to greet the day with enthusiasm and praise for the redeeming, restoring grace of Jesus, taking nothing for granted.

He stood in awe that his heart, once so empty and void, was now filled to overflowing. Some days it seemed he might burst with gratitude for all God had done; not only in his own life, but also in Jolene's.

Once they had settled on a date, Tom began to struggle with feelings of impatience. Tired of straddling the fence, he became increasingly anxious to share the news with their daughters. Yet he knew Jolene needed to be completely at peace with the timing of their announcement and for whatever reason she still seemed apprehensive about letting their secret out.

Upon questioning, she admitted her reluctance mainly stemmed from concern she wouldn't be able to properly relinquish the role she had been forced to take on as head of her own house after they had split apart. Biblical submission and marital oneness definitely weren't habits she'd fostered while living a fairly self-sufficient life as a single mom. Now that counseling had revealed just how deeply Tom longed to feel needed, she wondered if she would be able to sufficiently depend on him like she should.

So, as she grappled with those issues, Tom was forced to once again take on the role of an idling car, waiting for Jolene to accelerate the two of them forward at her own pace.

❧

Over Labor Day weekend, Jolene flew out to Napa Valley for a mini vacation with her sister. Besides providing much-needed bonding time for the two of them, it was a perfect opportunity for deep soul searching and uninterrupted prayer time as Jolene wrestled with some of her concerns and laid them out to her Father.

Just a few weeks before, Tom had been at her house helping dry dishes when she had first mentioned the possibility of going to California. He had later expressed just how much the interaction had meant to him. By her demeanor it had been clear the conversation wasn't to simply inform him of her decision or work out logistics for taking care of the girls while she was away. She had truly been seeking his advice and approval and would have been willing to heed whatever answer he gave. It had been another small but pivotal victory in their relationship as he had wholeheartedly supported her taking some time away to reflect on the future.

By the end of the trip she was bathed in peace each time she considered the prospect of moving ahead with Tom. It seemed the time had come. Fully realizing remarriage was a giant leap of faith, she simply rested in the reassuring knowledge her Lord would be there to "spot" her as she made the jump. No matter what happened, He would be faithful; of that she was fully convinced.

Arriving home Monday afternoon, there was unpacking and laundry to do, keeping her busy until bedtime. But Tuesday morning she called Tom and shared that she was finally prepared to announce to the world they were going to give marriage another chance.

Voicing those words sent an unforeseen thrill of anticipation through her. On the other end of the line Tom's heart began to race wildly as he pumped his fist in the air repeatedly before breaking into a prayer of praise to Jesus for His awesome faithfulness throughout their journey.

Desiring to tell Shelby, Shania, and Shayna before sharing the news with anyone else, they made arrangements for Tom to come up the following Sunday for church and dinner, where they would make the announcement to the girls.

Anxious to celebrate such a joyous occasion with the four most precious ladies in his life, waiting until Sunday seemed like an eternity to Tom. But he wasn't about to complain.

Just two days after making plans to tell the girls, Jolene called Tom in a panic. She had awoken that morning from a frightening dream. Although the details were already fuzzy in her mind, it had something to do with her and Tom and left her with an uneasiness she couldn't shake.

She was grateful for Tom's calm reassurance in response as he reminded her over and over it would be ok and she didn't need to fear her dream.

So, three days later she found herself at church, expectantly waiting for Tom to walk in. She wondered if her feelings of anticipation and excitement were evident to anyone who noticed her unusual interest in the doorway.

After church they all headed to Jolene's home for the afternoon. In spite of the life-altering secret they were about to share with their daughters, Tom and Jolene made a valiant attempt to appear nonchalant as all five lazed around that afternoon, until they finally gathered in the dining room for dinner.

Tom began the meal with a heartfelt prayer, although he could barely keep his voice from trembling with excitement. The girls innocently chattered while Tom and Jolene both ate in relative silence, deeply enjoying the normalcy of feeling like a "complete" family around the dinner table.

Finally, Tom could contain himself no longer, abruptly interrupting the girls' banter midstream. "Girls, your mom and I have something to ask you." Then he paused dramatically while everyone stared at him, waiting expectantly for him to pose what must be an important question.

Before they all exploded from the anticipation, he continued, "What would you think of me living here with all of you?"

Six eyes widened into saucers and mouths dropped open all around the table as one by one the girls set their forks down.

A slow smile began to spread across Jolene's face as she watched their daughters' reactions.

Shelby was the first to recover her voice. "Are you serious, Dad?"

Tom's eyes glinted mischievously. Glancing at Jolene he replied, "Have you ever heard your mom joke about getting married to Dad?"

All three girls looked at each other incredulously. Even seven-year-old Shayna knew Mom never, ever joked about her relationship with Daddy! He really must be serious!

Shania was the first to answer his question with an emphatic, "*No*, we haven't!" at the same time shaking her head vigorously for emphasis. She was fully aware her parents' relationship was no joking matter!

No sooner had Shania gotten the words out when Shayna suddenly jumped up, pushed her chair away from the table and rushed towards the door. Everyone watched her in confusion, unsure what she was doing or why she was reacting in such a manner.

Reaching the door, she flung it open, stuck her head outside and began to scream ecstatically.

While Tom and Jolene both erupted in hysterical laughter at Shayna's unbridled delight, her two older sisters immediately hushed her, mortified that the neighbors might hear her screams and label the whole family as weird. Shayna cooperated with her embarrassed sisters by closing the door but, unable to sit still, began skipping and bouncing around the table. Every now and then she would erupt with another shriek of delight. With a closed door protecting their reputation from being damaged, Shelby and Shania willingly overlooked her antics, even joining in with their own little squeals of excitement as they processed their dad's announcement.

After awhile, all three girls began peppering both parents with questions. When? How? Where? Finding out the wedding date was only seven weeks away brought further shrieks of happiness.

Eventually they calmed down enough to finish their meal then all worked together to clear the table and load the dishwasher before heading outside to the driveway for a family game of basketball.

As they played, a plane flew over, high above them. Referring to their plans to fly to the Dominican Republic for a second honeymoon, Tom pointed to it and casually commented to Jolene, "That's us in about seven weeks." His remark instantly made her queasy as panic rose up within her. She fought the urge to give in to her fears, reminding herself that this leap of faith wasn't easy but God was right there, holding her hand. He would be with her each step of the way. She was able to calm down fairly quickly but she found herself frustrated at the way her emotions still swung back and forth so wildly.

After Tom had left to head back home, Jolene called her dad and mom and invited them over. She let the girls break the news to them since they were bouncing up and down with excitement as soon as their grandparents' vehicle turned into the driveway. Jolene caught herself carefully scrutinizing her parents' faces to try and read their thoughts as they processed the news. All she detected was love and support.

Later that evening, she picked up the phone to call her siblings. As she hung up from the final call, she was extremely grateful for their reactions. There hadn't been the slightest hint of hesitation in any of their voices. In fact, they seemed authentically happy for her and Tom, which proved to be a tremendous relief.

Tom, too, was thankful for his parents' reaction when he called them. Because they were now living out of state they hadn't been able to witness the changes in him up close, nor had they seen his deepening relationship with Jolene. But after an initial, "Are you sure, Tom?" they gave their full support to his decision.

Over the course of the next few hours and even days, they found themselves enjoying and even slightly amused by the reactions of their friends and extended family as they spread word of their engagement. When Tom called his employer, who had also become a dear friend, to tell him he was engaged he definitely hadn't expected the response he received.

"Really? Who to?"

In fact, the more people they told the more they discovered there hadn't really been anyone who had realistically clung to any hope they would get back together. It seemed everyone had pretty much given up on their relationship.

Everyone, that is, except the Author and Finisher of life stories.

Throughout their courtship, Ron had warned Tom to be very careful in regards to physical touch. Even though they had once been married, and for all practical purposes still were in God's eyes, to the watching world – and especially their little girls – they were now divorced and needed to set an example of purity. Therefore Jolene had made it quite clear she desired a full commitment before there would be any physical touch whatsoever.

On the way to a family gathering at her brother's house a couple weeks into their engagement, Tom reached for Jolene's hand and gave a slight squeeze. She was pleasantly surprised by the little shiver that went through her at his gentle touch.

Immediately, they heard giggling from the backseat. Glancing in the rearview mirror, Tom couldn't help joining in with the laughter when he saw all three girls wildly motioning to one another and pointing at their parents' interlocked hands, pure delight written all over their young faces.

Plans began to fall into place for a small, simple ceremony. They were able to rent their church's Fellowship Center for the wedding as well as reception and arranged for Ron, their much-admired and appreciated counselor, who was also a minister, to help with the service. Her sister-in-law offered to make the cake. Aiming for an intimate gathering of those who had loved and supported them throughout the painful past seven or eight years, they only invited immediate family and grandparents, along with their closest friends

Desiring to make it an extra special event for their daughters, they wanted to find matching dresses for the three of them to wear as they walked down the aisle ahead of their mom. Finding something in all three sizes proved more difficult than they'd imagined and when they finally found the dresses, they centered the rest of their wedding colors on the pink shade of the girls' dresses.

Nervous about finding something for herself, Jolene began searching right away. She was delighted to find exactly what she was looking for after a very brief search online; a beautifully elegant, floor-length gown, with simple but traditional A-line styling from a modest bridal website. However, with a no-return policy she hesitated to place the order, concerned about the sizing. For a couple days she found herself repeatedly standing in the middle of her office, measuring and re-measuring. Finally, with the wedding day quickly approaching, she went ahead, typed in the measurements and hit submit, praying it would actually fit.

A week later when the package arrived, it definitely met, and even exceeded, her expectations, requiring only a minimal amount of altering from a dear friend in Tom's hometown. When she went for a final fitting, gratitude welled up within her for the care her friend had taken to fit the wedding dress so perfectly to her. Turning in a slow circle in front of the mirror, she had to admit she felt like a princess getting ready to marry her knight.

It was a radically different feeling than she'd had during her first wedding day preparations.

Although there were admittedly a few awkward moments as they adjusted to the newness of being a couple again, Tom and Jolene both found it to be a completely different experience than their first engagement period when questions had begun to arise in both of their hearts.

This time there was none of the apprehension, anxiety or uneasiness in the pit of their stomachs. Instead, they both had the sense of being blessed with a distinct opportunity to live out a miracle. Jolene was finally able to move beyond the nagging doubts. She was forever grateful for the wisdom and love of her mentor friend, who challenged her not to live in fear of the possibility Tom may leave her again. Speaking from her own experience, this friend gently explained to Jolene the importance of choosing to trust again, no matter how difficult it seemed. Because it is one of the most fundamental principles of love, a relationship must be built on trust in order to stand. In light of that, she frankly reminded Jolene that her days of playing detective were over from this point forward.

Through the accountability of her mentor and the knowledge that God had never once failed her before, Jolene was able to rest in the knowledge that if He had helped her weather the storms the first time around He would help her again, no matter what lay ahead.

She was fully confident of one thing.

Though Tom might fail her, God never would!

Chapter 22

*O*ctober 18, 2008 dawned a gloriously crisp, autumn day filled with the beauty of God's creation.

The world outside the windows reflected the artistic touch of the Almighty; a brilliant masterpiece of vibrant color painted across the landscape of the Midwest.

Inside, those gathered for the exchanging of vows between Tom and Jolene were eyewitnesses to another magnificent work of art crafted by His hand. All in attendance were keenly aware that no human was capable of creating such a beautiful, intact family out of the shattered pieces of two sinful humans' failures and mistakes. Without a doubt, what they were witnessing was truly the miraculous work of God alone.

As Tom stood in the front row watching his cherished daughters sweetly glide down the aisle one at a time, he was overcome with emotion. All the painful wounds his self-centeredness had caused his family, every one of his mistakes as a father, even his failure to be a faithful husband to their mom seemed to have been completely erased from his daughters' memories as they eagerly fixed their eyes on him with complete innocence and trust. As they made their way towards him, not one hint of resentment was evident anywhere on their faces. He was so proud to call these three little princesses his very own!

Sensitive, reserved ten-year-old Shelby came first. She locked her mature, gentle eyes on Tom as she made her way towards him. It seemed Shelby had grown up too quickly during his time away from the family. It nearly broke Tom's heart to imagine just how many moments had slipped through his selfish fingers during the separation; memories he could never gain back. Nine-year-old Shania followed close behind. Carefree and glowing with happiness, her outgoing nature was basking in the excitement of the moment. Above the dainty dress her sparkling eyes danced as she met her dad's tear-filled gaze and flashed him a spunky smile. Sweet little seven-year-old Shayna came last, eyes darting shyly from side to side at the faces on either side of the aisle. Then, focusing solely on her dad, she beamed at him below her rosy little cheeks. Receiving a reassuring grin in return, her chin lifted ever so slightly as she continued forward with greater confidence.

Many thoughts flashed through his mind at lightning speed as his daughters advanced down the aisle. But what touched his heart most deeply as he glanced at all three girls was the radiant smiles, not only on their lips, but also reflected in each one of their eyes. Intensely humbled by their childlike faith and forgiving hearts, he began to shake with sobs of gratitude and praise, not only for the undeserved redemption of His Savior but also the forgiveness and love of his precious family.

Christ truly *had* brought beauty from ashes, just like He said He would in Isaiah 61:3.

The three adorable girls were so charming in their full-length pink dresses gathered at the waist with a satin ribbon that they had commanded everyone's full attention. But now all eyes turned to look beyond Shayna to Jolene as a hush fell over the room. All was quiet, other than the strains of piano music floating over those gathered there.

A huge lump arose in Tom's throat at the beautiful sight of his bride approaching in her white dress. With slate wiped clean, all things had become new and she was a pure bride adorned for him, her husband!

Jolene's gaze, fixed intently on him as she slowly walked forward, spoke volumes to his heart. Tom saw in her countenance an abiding faith and trust. He knew beyond a shadow of a doubt her confidence was in Someone much greater than him, just as it should be. That thought brought him deep comfort.

As she reached him and they turned together to face Ron, cleansing tears of joy coursed down his cheeks. All he could think of was his unworthiness...and yet at the same time he was overwhelmed by a profound gratefulness for Jesus, Who had loved him enough to relentlessly pursue him until he was truly ready to be found.

Almost twelve years prior, at their first wedding, Jolene's crying had deeply troubled Tom. Sitting beside her throughout that ceremony, he had been alarmed as rivers of tears flowed down her face. In his insecurity he had wondered what she found so dreadful about marrying him that she couldn't even smile on her wedding day. Not once had he considered what a highly emotional time it was for her as she prepared to say goodbye to life as she knew it; her family, friends, home, town, church, job, and everything else that had become familiar to her in twenty years of life. Instead, he had taken her tears personally and allowed Satan to wedge his foot in the door right there during their ceremony.

In contrast, it was now Tom fighting wave after wave of emotion while Jolene remained calm and peaceful at his side. Rather than being wounded by his tears, she was touched by how deeply he cared and how seriously he seemed to be taking the marriage commitment this time around.

They were blessed by an excellent wedding service, based on 1 Corinthians 13, in which Ron focused on the "attitude" of love as well as the choices it involves. Challenging them never to be suspicious of one another, but to always believe the best about the other one, Ron also reminded them they would eventually fail each other because of their humanness. But, if they could learn to live it out correctly, love itself would not fail, according to verse 8. And although they would never be able to completely forget the past, he encouraged them they didn't have to relive or overanalyze it. Nor were they expected to understand why life had unfolded the way it had for the two of them. In fact, God sometimes allows mysteries in life without expecting or even allowing His people to grasp the full meaning while living here on earth: "For now we see through a glass darkly; but then face to face: now I know in part, but then shall I know even as also I am known." (1 Cor. 13:12 KJV)

One of the most touching moments in the service occurred when Ron looked at Shelby, Shania, and Shayna sitting in the front row. "Is today exciting to you?" he kindly questioned with a smile, receiving emphatic nods in return. He then told them, "Someday you will understand this day differently than you do now. This is about so much more than the excitement of getting all dressed up, or having daddy come home again. It is way bigger than all of that. When you grow up you will understand your parents made an incredible decision here today to love each other."

His comment sent fresh tears streaming down Tom's cheeks.

Soon it was time for Tom and Jolene to stand and join right hands together as they took their wedding vows. Though they were simply stated, the promises made that day held much deeper significance for both of them than they had on that sunny winter day in February of 1997. This time, as they pledged faith-fulness to one another from this day forward, they did not do so naively. Although life had taught them just how easily vows can be broken, they had also learned just how strong the grip of God's grace. They both had full confidence their marriage would endure the test of time *if*—and only if—they each relied on Christ daily for the strength to be whom He had called them to be individually, and then together as a couple.

In a breathtaking, beautiful moment they were announced husband and wife once again. In spite of all the pain, hurt and division, their union had been fully restored by the grace of God. Though man had deemed them irreconcilable, God had proven different:

"Reconcilable Differences."

Without a doubt, differences still remained between the two of them, but they no longer believed the differences were beyond the scope of God's ability to resolve and help them work through.

Jolene had remained strong throughout the ceremony, but her emotions eventually hit with a vengeance during the receiving line. As one after another of their family and friends placed tender arms around them with kind assurances of their prayerful concern and love, her heart was moved with thankfulness and a sense of humble inadequacy. This time, Tom welcomed the tears he saw on her cheeks as they stood hand in hand acknowledging each guest.

Without a doubt, as uncomfortable as their first wedding had been, their second wedding day proved to be the exact opposite. Discussing it later, Tom and Jolene could find no better words to describe that day more appropriately than "phenomenal" and even "magical". At ease, relaxed and peaceful, they had both enjoyed every single moment.

With plans to spend a few days at home with the girls prior to leaving for a honeymoon, they had felt no pressure to rush off from the reception, instead relishing in every moment with their guests. In fact, when it was time to leave they didn't leave alone; all the out of town friends and family followed Tom and Jolene to their house for a tour, while her family and the girls stayed behind to clean up.

Showing their house and then saying goodbyes to everyone took longer than expected. As Tom and Jolene were standing together in the driveway bidding farewell to the last of their guests, Jolene's parents drove in with Shelby, Shania and Shayna.

Hopping out of the vehicle, the three girls ran right past their parents and up the deck stairs, obviously up to something. Tom and Jolene took their time walking slowly across the deck and into the house with hands intertwined.

They were barely inside the door before they heard three precious voices calling from the living room. There a piece of cake sat awaiting each of them on the coffee table. A simple gesture, yet it sent a fresh flood of praise through them both as they relished in the delight of their girls and the awe of what God had done in their lives. Just two weeks shy of eight years from the day their family unit had been torn apart, against all odds here they were all back together under one roof again!

To top off a glorious day, the five of them sat snuggled together on the couch, sharing cake and opening the cards they had been given, cherishing each word.

Suddenly the girls started whispering and giggling together. Tom winked at Jolene, guessing what it was all about. Pretty soon Shelby was standing in front of them with a camera while all three girls began coaxing their parents to kiss. As Tom obliged the girls, Shayna bounced up and down excitedly. In between bounces she burst out in delight, assuring Tom that since he and mommy were married now, he could finally spend the night at their house! In her most hospitable tone, she went on to inform him they would even make him a bed on the couch. Laughing good-naturedly, Tom patted Shayna on the head while sneaking a sideways glance at Jolene. He was relieved to see the twinkle in her eye and marveled again at how beautifully natural everything about this day had been.

Following four blissful days of family togetherness and irreplaceable memories, just the two of them headed to Punta Cana, Dominican Republic for an amazing honeymoon. Again, both were in complete awe at the ease of their companionship. It was like a dream come true as they relaxed together, shared their hopes and dreams for the future and basked in the tropical rays of sunshine. There was such a warm sense of being personally blessed by their Heavenly Father in every way imaginable; from the delicious food they were served, the luxury of the resort, the matchless beauty of the beach, perfect weather, and most of all the effortlessness of their relationship; every little detail seemed to have been personally poured out by the Lord into their lives as His wedding gift!

At the end of a wonderful week they were ready to return home to their girls and begin the joy of living together the way God had intended them to from the very beginning of their first marriage.

It was time to put their new tools to the test. The honeymoon was over and soon would come the moment of truth.

Could they walk the walk in daily life?

Chapter 23

$\mathcal{I}$t didn't take long for Tom and Jolene to discover a rather obvious but nonetheless harsh reality about their marriage: In spite of each having a much more intimate relationship with Jesus than they had their first marriage, they were not immune to conflict. Contrary to popular belief, being vibrant Christians doesn't automatically guarantee a problem-free marriage.

Many couples see conflict as something to be avoided at all costs. In truth, the presence of conflict isn't the main culprit of damaged or dead relationships. Conflict is simply a reality of life. It is the way in which conflict is handled that can either make or break the relationship. Couples with healthy marriages don't have zero conflict; they've just learned to effectively and respectfully deal with it as it arises.

The first time tension rose between Tom and Jolene after their honeymoon, some of their instinctual responses from days gone by immediately began to rear up from deep within. But as evidence of God's amazing grace at work in their lives, they each were quick to recognize and squelch the wrong attitudes before they were allowed to have the upper hand. Instead of beginning to accumulate the old familiar pile of baggage under a brand new rug, they respectfully and lovingly dealt with the issue and mutually worked through it by implementing many of the tools they had learned through counseling.

Though they had already had their share of positive rein-forcement during their time of courting, both had worried if things would be different once they were married and had let their guard down a little. Instead, they were pleasantly sur-prised to find that they had diffused this first tense situation even better than expected. As Jolene pondered the difference in how Tom had handled the circumstances she couldn't help but be in awe. Rather than running from the problem or erupting with a raised voice, he had portrayed great maturity and grace. The words he'd spoken had been seasoned with salt.

Similarly, Jolene's reaction had not escaped Tom's notice. In the past her normal response might have been to confront him in an accusing tone but this time she had immediately taken responsibility for her share of the issue, asking his forgiveness and listening rationally as he explained the way he'd felt and why he had been bothered by her actions.

That night, lying in bed next to one another they sensed they had won a great victory, together. But not naïve newlyweds the second time around, they knew that this was just one of many battles to come. If only they could always keep in mind who the real enemy was and never allow him to divide and conquer!

Just as important as clearly identifying their enemy was always keeping in mind where their strength came from. Without a doubt, it was Christ alone who had turned their relationship around. Sure, there were practical steps they had each taken, and needed to continue implementing on a daily basis in order to foster better communication and interactions. But even those required dependence upon the continual grace of God. Human nature tends to be self-seeking at the core, unless held in check. Both had learned that if left to themselves their flesh would eventually grow weary and return to being self-absorbed.

Because of their unusual story of reconciliation, Tom and Jolene both began to find themselves in the position to answer questions and help other couples in hurting or broken marriages. Many times Tom would be asked what he believed to have been the root issue in their first marriage. It never took him long to come up with an answer. In his mind, *selfishness* had been the source of the majority of their problems. Rather than seeking to understand Jolene he now realized he had been demanding and harsh in his expectations of her. In stark contrast the second time around, he was intentionally modeling his role as a husband after Christ's sacrificial love for His bride, the Church.

Jolene, on the other hand, realized she had gone into marriage eleven years prior unrealistically thinking she would be able to change all the areas of Tom's life she didn't particularly care for. In response, whenever he didn't meet her expectation of a godly husband or best friend she had done her best to transform him into the man she wanted him to be. Unfortunately, they had both grown deeply frustrated in the process. Not long into their second marriage she heard wise words which had struck a chord within her and became a guiding principle for her relationship with Tom.

"If your expectations aren't being met, maybe it's time to change your expectations."

Many of the issues that had eroded their marriage started out extremely small and tended to be nothing more than petty annoyances that had grown out of hand. Tom and Jolene had definitely learned many lessons during their time apart. They now prayed regularly for grace to properly implement the tools with which they had been equipped. Most of the "tools" were merely practical, common sense anyway.

As one year melted into another, they continued to learn more about each other as well as themselves. Fully dedicated to continually improving their marriage in any way possible, they attended a FamilyLife Weekend to Remember prior to their second anniversary. At the conference they soaked up truths and tools to improve and maintain a vibrant and healthy relationship. Learning to appreciate their differences rather than viewing them as negative, they headed home refreshed and renewed in their commitment to live intentionally; moving towards one-ness, rather than the inevitable drift towards isolation.

Determined to make this second marriage the best it could be, and out of mutual love and respect for one another, Tom and Jolene came up with a handful of simple foundational rules they were both committed to living by from this point forward:

They would seek to honor God in every way, but especially in their marriage relationship. Because it served as a picture in the flesh of His relationship with His children, they desired their marriage to be a reflection of grace, forgiveness and uncondi-tional love to a watching world.

They would be extremely careful to live lives of integrity, doing nothing to destroy each other's trust in any way. This meant they would carefully guard their actions, never giving a reason for the other one to question their faithfulness. Nor would they live in doubt or suspicion of one another.

Intentionally speaking one another's love language and keeping their spouse's tank filled would be of utmost impor-tance. For Jolene this meant building Tom up through verbal affirmations. Tom realized he needed to make time with Jolene a priority in order that she always felt truly loved.

Communication would be done in such a way that never tore one another down. Healthy communication also includes good listening skills; truly hearing what the other is trying to say, even the unspoken words and body language. So they would practice listening with their heart as well as their ears. And then they would graciously give each other the opportunity to respond, holding fast to the rule to always speak the truth in love.

Neither one would speak negatively about the other to anyone. Period.

They would embrace their differences as a positive piece of God's plan, not a problematic part of their relationship.

Dating one another would be a carefully guarded priority in life. Choosing to invest time in their relationship, they took turns planning monthly dates, often surprising the other one with a creative outing. Other times they spent a relaxing evening at home in the hot tub or simply sitting on the deck, talking and enjoying an evening together. Regardless of the activity, the thought and time spent in preparation became a gift in itself that was much more valuable than the dollar amount spent. Being resourceful, they sometimes planned lunch dates rather than dinner, because it was less expensive and fit their schedules better.

Instead of having separate hobbies which drew them apart from one another, Tom and Jolene sought out mutual activities to participate in as a couple, such as snowmobiling, golf, tennis, riding bikes, and fishing. Learning to embrace the other's passions, they joined each other in watching chick flicks as well as football. The key was simply being together.

With time they began to notice other changes in their marriage, areas in which their fierce determination not to repeat mistakes from their past was producing healthier habits than the first time around.

Based on her growing understanding of him, Jolene became much more purposeful about making Tom feel needed and wanted. She had come to realize how essential it was for him to know he was a priority in her life so she worked hard to demonstrate that fact to him, ensuring he no longer had reason to feel he was playing second fiddle to anyone besides Christ.

Recognizing physical needs as well as emotional was an important factor for both of them and they determined together that physical intimacy would never again be used as a means of manipulation or selfishly withheld from each other. It was critical they strive to meet one another's needs regularly as an important safeguard of fidelity within their marriage.

In addition, Jolene resolved not to be a dream dasher. She would be deliberate in supporting and encouraging his ambitions and goals, no matter how outlandish they seemed to her. Ever the practical one, there had been plenty of times in the past when she had unknowingly shattered his dreams and wounded his confidence in one fell swoop. What she hadn't realized was that being undermined in this area chipped away at Tom's willingness to lead the home in other areas. In contrast, by expressing her belief in his dreams she gave him the confidence to be the man God called him to be.

From the moment he had watched his daughters and Jolene walk down the aisle towards him with so much trust on their faces, Tom had been committed to becoming a true spiritual leader in their home. Not in word only, but also in deed. Jolene quickly grew to respect his leadership, witnessing God at work in his life as head of their home. She was blessed as she considered how drastically he had changed; he was more spiritual, less religious – polar opposite from how she would have described him during their first marriage.

In another radical change of behavior, whenever Tom needed some downtime to recharge, Jolene purposely refused to make him feel guilty. More than that, she had come to learn from their counselor that men often need a "man cave" to retreat to when they feel threatened. Whenever he goes into that cave, be it a physical room he escapes to or just an emotional place of refuge, it is the woman's job not to follow him. Ron had compared it to a dragon going into his lair. If you follow him in, you're going to get burned. It was a word picture Jolene could relate to all too well. In their previous marriage whenever Tom had retreated to the workshop to tinker, Jolene had instinctively pursued him, only to find herself often leaving his "lair" with her heart singed.

Now she realized she needed to give him time to cool off in solitude. She grew to appreciate his "man cave", knowing when he had calmed down and felt ready he would come find her so they could maturely discuss whatever issue needed to be. Until then, she needed to give him space and patiently wait.

Probably one of the most profound changes for them stemmed from a subtle but critical shift in perspective towards marriage itself. Once they came to recognize marriage as a gift from their Heavenly Father, each considered the other one to be a handpicked present from the Lord. To not appreciate one's spouse as a gift is to not appreciate the Giver. This mindset deepened their gratitude for each other, as well as for the Gift-giver, immensely!

As they celebrated their sixth wedding anniversary on October 18, 2014 there was a deep sense of joy in knowing, by God's grace, they had sustained their second marriage longer than they had suffered through the painful first one! In six years' time they had learned so much about each other, themselves, and Jesus. Not all the lessons had been easy—or lessons they would have chosen to learn—but each one had been for their good and God's glory.

Throughout it all, they were both fully aware without the spirit of Christ dwelling in them, each of the positive changes in their marriage would have been incredibly difficult, if not impossible to implement. But with the One who is defined as "Love" living within them, their marriage simply became a stunning reflection of Christ's love for His Bride, the Church.

One day Tom was struck with a sense of melancholy he just couldn't shake, in spite of multiple attempts. Finally he gave in to the beckoning call of introspection. Looking back over his life, he couldn't help but grieve a little, as he always did when he considered the meandering path he had journeyed down before arriving at the point where he was today.

Sadly, he understood all too personally the depth of truth in the popular saying, **"Sin will take you further than you want to go, keep you longer than you want to stay, and cost you more than you ever meant to pay."** Those words deeply resonated in his soul, bringing with them a godly sorrow as he considered just how far Satan had caused him to sink, then held him captive to selfishness way too long at an exorbitant cost to himself as well as all those he dearly loved.

But before the burden of his past could seize hold of his heart and weigh him down, he was taken by another memory. He had recently attended a business networking meeting where a phrase he'd heard had struck him profoundly. Recalling it now brought a joy to his heart that far surpassed the earlier weight of his remembered sin.

"A pencil has an eraser for a reason...but it also has a sharp point to write over mistakes after they have been erased."

As soon as the speaker had said it, Tom was moved by the analogy.

Wasn't that just like Jesus? Not only is He full of grace and forgiveness, blotting out our transgressions with His cleansing blood, but He also steps in with brand new mercies every morning as He goes about the business of authoring a new story far beyond our wildest imagination.

Today, as Satan tried to bludgeon Tom with memories of the past, he was deeply grateful for God's pencil. What a blessing to have the assurance God had graciously erased all the wretched mistakes from his life so they no longer had any power over him! Greater still was the comforting thought that even now, from His throne in Heaven, his Father was busily writing over every one with a narrative so much more glorious and grand than anything Tom would have ever envisioned on his own.

And better yet, Tom realized the half had not yet been told in his and Jolene's lives.

Because, for Believers, *the best is yet to come!*

Afterword

———✦✕✦———

*I*t has been said, "**God can heal a broken heart, but He has to have all the pieces.**"

How many times do we, as Christians, shake our raised hands at God in exasperation, asking Him why He hasn't put our broken hearts and lives back together again...when in fact those very hands we raise are cut and bleeding from the broken shards to which we are still desperately clinging? Even as we accuse Him of working too slowly, the shattered pieces dig ever deeper into our tightly clenched fists.

He is capable of bringing healing beyond our imagination, but He will never force His way. He wants us to willingly open our hands, one finger at a time—if that's what it takes—placing every last splinter at His feet. Then, and only then, will He do His mighty work. Too often we resist relinquishing every last piece into His All-Sufficient hands, not realizing our stubbornness is the very reason we continue in our misery.

For Tom and Jolene, the healing of their marriage didn't come until they had each individually opened wide their hands and released every single piece to Him. If your marriage has not yet been healed, I encourage you to open your hands. Is there still some piece you are foolishly clutching? Trust me, my friend; there is no greater Healer than Jehovah. Trust and believe Psalm 147:3: "He heals the brokenhearted and binds up their wounds." And Isaiah 61:1–3, a beautiful chapter which Christ used to declare His purpose in coming to earth: "The Spirit of the Lord God is upon me, because the LORD has anointed me to preach good tidings to the poor; He has sent me to heal the brokenhearted, to proclaim liberty to the captives, and the opening of the prison to them that are bound." He is able. He just waits for you to relinquish it all into His all-capable hands.

Perhaps you have placed all the pieces down before Him but your estranged spouse has not. Diligently pray that he or she will open his or her hands and pour everything out. Only then will Jehovah-Rapha (The LORD heals) begin the work He alone can do. Never give up. He is in the restoration business and He is unsurpassed in what He does!

Additional Resources:

Apostolic Christian Counseling and Family Services:

515 E Highland Street

Morton, IL 61550

309-263-5536

877-370-9988

www.accounseling.org

FamilyLife Weekend to Remember Marriage Conference:

http://www.familylife.com/weekend

800-358-6329

Five Love Languages

By Dr. Gary Chapman

http://www.5lovelanguages.com/

Reconcilable Differences Facebook page:

Administered by Tom and Jolene Young

To stay in touch with Tom and Jolene go to facebook.com/

ReconcilableDifferences/community

Rejoice Marriage Ministries

http://www.rejoiceministries.org/